OREGON'S MOST NOTORIOUS CRIMES

OREGON'S MOST NOTORIOUS CRIMES

1900-1955

MARGARET LAPLANTE

AMERICA THROUGH TIME®

ADDING COLOR TO AMERICAN HISTORY

America Through Time is an imprint of Fonthill Media LLC
www.through-time.com
office@through-time.com

Published by Arcadia Publishing by arrangement with Fonthill Media LLC
For all general information, please contact Arcadia Publishing:
Telephone: 843-853-2070
Fax: 843-853-0044
E-mail: sales@arcadiapublishing.com
For customer service and orders:
Toll-Free 1-888-313-2665

www.arcadiapublishing.com

First published 2022

ISBN 978-1-63499-386-9

Typeset in 10.5pt on 13pt Sabon
Printed and bound in England

Contents

Introduction

Long before Oregon was actually a state, there was crime. In the early days, fur trappers and explorers came through the area. Later, the Donation Land Claim Act and the Gold Rush brought thousands of people to what would become the state of Oregon. With people in search of the same thing, be it furs, land, or gold, tensions ran high. Frequently, criminals were not afforded due process, and many hangings took place before questions were asked. The first courtrooms were sometimes just a table in a store. The first jail in Oregon was located in Oregon City. In 1851, the Oregon State Penitentiary opened in Portland. Fifteen years later, it moved to Salem, where it has been ever since. For the first century, there was only one prison in Oregon.

1

The Lava Lake Murders

In 1924, three men were reported missing in Deschutes County. The missing trio were Ed Nichols, age fifty-five; Roy Wilson, age thirty-five; and Dewey Morris, age thirty. Their relatives reported that the men never returned from a trapping expedition in the mountains surrounding Bend.

A search party consisting of twenty men combed the mountains south of Bend from April 14–16, 1924. When they failed to turn up anything of significance, Sheriff Roberts asked Deputy Sheriff C. A. Adams, who was also the district game warden, to join in the search. Dewey Morris' brothers, Donald and Ben, joined Deputy Sheriff Adams in the search of the three missing men.

A search near the cabin where they were staying revealed a blood-stained sled. Two of the men's coats were in the cabin, making the searchers believe they left against their will. The searchers also noticed that several valuable fox pelts were missing. Their cabin was on the shore of Lava Lake. The sheriff became increasingly concerned that the men may have tried to cross the ice of the Crane Prairie reservoir. He feared that if they had attempted to cross the ice, they could have fallen through.

Deputy Sheriff Adams and Deputy Sheriff George Stokoe headed to Klamath County to do additional research on the stolen fox pelt. Their investigation revealed that one fox pelt had been sold in Klamath County in the middle of January. Additionally, four fox pelts had been sold to Schumaker Fur Store located at Third and Main Streets in Portland. Multnomah County Sheriff Hurlburt spoke with the proprietor of the Schumaker Fur Store and learned that someone using a trapper card belonging to E. D. Nichols of Bend, Oregon, had sold the furs on January 22, 1924. The description of the fur seller was that he was about 5 feet 7 inches and weighed approximately 150 pounds. The seller wore a beaver hat and khaki clothing. The seller told the clerk that he had been trapping in the Packsaddle Mountain area of the central Oregon Cascades. The clerk did say that the pelts were in extremely bad condition, having been skinned by someone inexperienced or who was in a hurry. The sheriff was unable to determine if it was Ed or someone using Ed's card who sold the furs.

Meanwhile, back on the lake, the searchers saw a large hole in the lake with what appeared to be a human hair on the jagged edge of the hole. They wanted to get a closer look at the hole but they were afraid that the ice would not hold. They decided to send Ed Logan onto the lake because he weighed the least. They tied a lifeline around his waist and he made his way towards the hole in the ice. Once on the ice, he discovered there were numerous soft spots on the ice so he had to turn back. They decided to wait until the ice broke up.

Finally, when the ice broke, Sheriff Roberts ordered a motor boat to search the reservoir. Deputy Sheriff C. A. Adams, H. D. Innis, and Ed Logan were tasked with searching Lava Lake. Once on the water, it did not take long to see three bodies floating side by side. Two of the men did not have a coat on. The searchers located a hat on the ice and noticed that two of the men still had their hats on. Ed still had his glasses on. The bodies were located 100 feet inshore from the hole that had been cut in the ice.

The next day members of the search party assisted in retrieving the bodies from Lava Lake. Those who helped included; Jerome Ward, Ray Ward, Bill Ruark, Owen Morris, Ben Morris, Donald Morris, H. D. Innis, Paul Hosmer, R.W. Sawyer, Myron Symons, Deputy Sheriff Adams, and Coroner C. P. Niswonger. D. W. Duffy of La Pine brought a wagon and team of horses to transport the bodies from the lake to the road where they met Einar Meistad of Bend. He in turn placed the bodies in his truck and took them to Bend.

The authorities surmised that the men had been forced to leave their cabin, were shot to death, and then dumped into Big Lava Lake through the large hole that had been cut in the ice. Law enforcement immediately narrowed in on one suspect—Charles Kimzey, alias Lee Collins. Kimzey, who at the time was an escapee from an Idaho state prison farm, was already wanted by Deschutes County Sheriff's Office for an assault on W. E. Harrison.

The investigators learned Kimzey had been in a confrontation over a stolen wallet with one of the three trappers previously. This only added to Sheriff Robert's belief that Kimzey was responsible for killing the three men.

The men were buried in adjoining graves at Greenwood cemetery. Reverend F. H. Beard conducted the burial with only close friends and relatives in attendance. Within days of the discovery of the bodies, Deschutes County offered a $1,500 reward for the murderer or murderers.

The grand jury was impaneled and listened intently to several witnesses. First on the witness stand was county physician, R. W. Henderson. He testified that Ed had been shot in the jaw. He had a bullet from a revolver in his side. Roy had been shot in the right shoulder and behind his right ear. Dewey had been shot in the elbow, but his cause of death was from a blunt instrument to the head. He had a hole about the size of a half dollar behind his ear. Henderson believed that Dewey had been shot in the forearm and was able to escape, only to be captured and beaten with a hammer. He believed two men were responsible for the murders. He was questioned about the length of time the men were in the lake. He told the grand jury it would be impossible to determine exactly how long, but he believed they had been in the water for at least one month.

Next to testify before the grand jury was Roy's brother-in-law, H. D. Innes. He recalled for the jury how he had arrived at the cabin along with Deputy Sheriff Adams and Ed Logan. He saw blood in the snow near the cabin, but there was no evidence of a struggle inside the cabin. He was asked if any of the trappers had enemies, to which he replied in the negative. He said when he was at the cabin the previous October, there had been seven guns but two weapons were now missing. He said that the traps had not been checked in quite some time and were full.

Ed Logan testified to seeing the hole in the ice on the lake as well as what he saw at the cabin. He explained that at the cabin he found empty shotgun shells 12 feet from the cabin. He said the snow was stained with blood in two spots. He believed that was where Roy and Dewey had been murdered. He believed that Ed was killed in the area where a fragment of a bone or tooth had been recovered due to his having been shot in the jaw. He did say they had located a hat in the cabin that was too large for any of the three trappers and it was from a store in Portland so they had seized it as evidence.

Deputy Sheriff Adams corroborated previous testimony when he took the stand. He testified that the empty shells corresponded to one of the missing weapons, a .38 caliber Luger, which was still in the cabin. When asked about a motive for the triple homicide, Deputy Sheriff Adams said he knew of one man who might want revenge and that was Charles Kimzey.

The grand jury returned the following verdict:

> In the matter of the deaths of Ed Nichols, Roy Wilson, and Dewey Morris, deceased. We the jury empaneled and sworn to inquire into the cause of the death of the above-named deceased persons, find that they all came to their death about the 15th day of January 1924, in the following manner: Ed Nichols was killed by a shotgun wound. Roy Wilson was killed by a bullet wound through the head. He was also shot with a shotgun. Dewey Morris was killed by being hit in the head with some blunt instrument. He was also shot with a shotgun. All these men were killed by a person or persons unknown to this jury.[1]

The verdict was signed by Foreman A. B. Taylor, Leroy Fox, Ora D. Allingham, La Vorn Taylor, and William Box.

Sheriff Roberts sent a fragment of the wood stained with blood from the sled for testing. He received a telegram from Melvin R. L. Benson, pathologist at the University of Oregon Medical School in Portland. The telegram read, "Stain on wood gives test for human blood."

In the beginning, the sheriff's office received a number of tips. They were not able to substantiate anything, and time began to pass without any more valuable information. Suddenly, a year went by, then another and another, yet the murders remained unsolved.

Finally, in 1933, Charles was arrested in Kalispell, Montana. By that time, Sheriff McCauley had put more than 10,000 miles on his patrol vehicle searching for Charles in what he referred to as "wild goose chases." Charles was extradited to Oregon to answer for the murders of the three trappers. He was held in the jail in Bend. What no one working at the jail could have imagined was that the townsfolk were so anxious to catch a glimpse of Charles, they were willing to spend ten cents to do so. Charles' cellmate, Joe Allen, was serving time for a liquor law violation during Prohibition. The two men came up with a system that when a citizen approached the window, Joe collected the dime and then Charles would come up to the window. By the time the staff realized what was happening, the two had made enough money to purchase a number of jigsaw puzzles. Joe was moved to the city jail, thus ending their business partnership.

Charles waived his preliminary hearing and was ordered to be held for investigation. Charles claimed he had been working on the Moffatt tunnel in Colorado in 1924. While the authorities were waiting on confirmation of this, Sheriff Claude McCauley took Charles to Portland in the hopes that someone at the Schumaker Fur Store could identify him as the man who sold the fox pelts almost a decade prior. They had previously seen a photograph of Charles and confirmed he was the man who sold the fox pelts to them. Additionally, Portland traffic officer W. C. Bender had positively identified Charles as the person who asked him for directions to a "reliable fur trader." Officer Bender said the man had a burlap bag slung over his shoulder. Officer Bender referred him to the Schumaker Fur Store.

During Charles' trial for assault and battery, W. E. testified that he was working as a taxicab driver when Charles hired him to take him to the high desert. Once there, W. E. threatened him with a gun, hit him over the head with a gun, forced him to drink poison, bound his hands and feet with wire, and tossed him into a dry well. W. E. said he vomited up the poison, was able to free himself from the wires, and climb out of the well. Once on solid ground, he discovered that Charles had stolen his car. He walked to a nearby ranch and was able to get help there. Judge T. E. J. Duffy said, "Never in all my time on the bench, have I listened to such a list of harrowing details in connection with a crime."

District Attorney Bert Boylan told Judge Duffy that Charles was a suspect in the slaying of the three trappers. Beyond that, no testimony was given regarding that crime. Two of the material witnesses decided at the last minute not to testify. Portland Police Officer Bender said he could no longer positively identify Charles. The owner of the fur shop, Carl Schumaker, did not think he could identify the suspect after so much time had passed. Charles was sentenced to life imprisonment for the assault with a weapon on W. E. Harrison. It was his fourth conviction. The following week he exited the county jail, handcuffed to Sheriff McCauley ready to be transported to prison. He smiled and nodded to the small crowd that had gathered.

Twelve years after he was sentenced, Charles escaped while working on a prison labor gang at the state prison farm. At the time of the escape, he was sixty years old. His time as a free man was short lived. Within a week, he was back behind bars after being spotted walking on a road near the prison by off duty prison guard Donald Johnson.

Time marched on, the tips became fewer and fewer, until they stopped all together. The Lava Lake murders remain unsolved. In 1927, Three Trappers Butte, a volcanic cone, was named in honor of Dewey Morris, Ed Nichols, and Roy Wilson.

2

Crater Lake National Park Murder Mystery

The morning of July 19, 1952, dawned under a bright blue sky. It was going to be warm in the Rogue Valley, but up at Crater Lake National Park, the temperature was going to be a pleasant 71 degrees.

Charles Patrick Culhane, age fifty-three, and Albert Marston Jones, age fifty-six, were on their way to Crater Lake National Park driving a 1951 green Pontiac sedan bearing California license plate 6A 16762. They checked in at the park entrance and paid the $1 admittance fee. Park Ranger Richard Marquiss wrote out their park pass and waved them through. It would be the last time anyone saw the men alive.

Charles was the national general sales manager for United Motors Service, a subsidy of General Motors, based in Detroit, Michigan. He was visiting the west coast and calling on businesses along with Albert who was the western sales manager for General Motors. Both men were well paid executives who were extremely dedicated to their profession. Charles was making $15,000 a year at a time when salaries were a quarter of that. Charles had a wife, Irene, and two grown sons—Charles, Jr., age twenty-three, and David, age twenty-one.

Albert began his career as a bond salesman in Seattle. At one point, he was part owner of Willis-Jones Tool Company. At the height of the Great Depression, he ended up bankrupt but managed to pay all of his creditors. Albert divorced his first wife, Alice, in 1950 and married for the second time soon after. His second wife, Orillia (Betty), also worked for United Motors Service. Albert and Alice had one grown daughter, Virginia, who lived in San Diego. Albert had a $20,000 life insurance policy.

In the days leading up to their trip to Crater Lake, the men had been visiting businesses in Albert's sales area. They arrived in Klamath Falls on Saturday, July 18, 1952, about 10 a.m. They met with F. W. Eberlein and John A. Vaughn at their business, Specialized Service Company. Their company was an auto parts business that had dealings with United Motors Service. The four men discussed going fishing at Union Creek that evening. Charles said that he was not feeling well and was not interested in fishing. The arrangement was that Charles and Albert would drive to Crater Lake and spend the afternoon there. Albert would meet F. W. and John at Crater Lake, and the three of them would head to Union Creek for an evening fishing trip. Charles would drive the Pontiac to Medford and spend Sunday taking care of some business. Albert would spend the night in Klamath Falls and then catch the bus to Medford on Monday morning and meet up with Charles. They would then resume calling on businesses.

At 11:15 a.m., Charles and Albert got back into the Pontiac and headed for Crater Lake. F. W. and John remained at their auto parts business until noon when they shut down for the day. They picked up F. W.'s twelve-year-old son, Alan, and headed out for their fishing trip. They arrived at Crater Lake at 2:45 p.m. They paid the admittance fee and began driving into the park. They were surprised to see the Pontiac parked near Annie Creek. They pulled in behind the Pontiac. They figured Charles and Albert had gone for a walk. However, they were bothered by the fact that one car door was wide open and the key was still in the ignition. They could see that the men's suitcases were untouched in the back. They called out for Charles and Albert but received no response.

At 3:50 p.m., when there was still no sign of the men, F. W., John, and Alan drove to the ranger station and explained the situation. The Park Rangers immediately began searching the canyon, fearing the men had had a terrible accident. They had not had any success by the time nightfall came. They ended the search with plans to begin again at dawn. Early the next morning, Chief Ranger Lou Hallock phoned the Oregon State Police. Chief Ranger Hallock explained that two men were missing and he feared they had fallen down the canyon. The Oregon State Police sent one trooper with the understanding that they would send more if the need arose. The search team worked well into the night but there was no sign of the men.

The following day, Monday, July 21, 1952, at 12:50 p.m., the search party led by Charles Kasling located Charles and Albert. They had been killed execution-style in a heavily wooded area approximately two-thirds of a mile from where their car was parked. As the murders occurred in a National Park, the FBI had jurisdiction. They arrived on scene and took over the investigation. James B. Poster, chief of the Portland office was the special agent in charge of the investigation.

Albert had been shot behind the ear on the left-hand side. His skull had been fractured, possibly from the butt of a gun. Charles had been shot through the right cheek. The men were lying face up, about 2 feet apart and at right angles to each other. Both men had been gagged with pieces of an undershirt, thought to belong to Charles. Their neckties had been used to hold the gags in place. The men's shoes had been removed and Albert's shoes were missing. The bottom of their socks were clean, meaning that they had not walked after their shoes were removed. The F.B.I. believed the men had been forced from their car into another car and driven to where their bodies were discovered. Special agents with the F.B.I. located two spent bullet cartridges near the bodies.

It was thought that one of the men had $300 in his wallet but the money was missing. A Shell Oil credit card was missing from Albert's wallet. Both of the men had been wearing expensive watches that were missing. The F.B.I. surmised that robbery had been the motive for the murders. The F.B.I. did some research and learned that Albert's watch was a Hamilton Drake model. It had a 10-carat gold filled case with number 0829452. It was inscribed on the back, "To A.M. Jones from UMS." Culhane's watch was believed to be a model made in America, with gold Arabic numerals.

At 1:15 p.m. that day, a mere twenty-five minutes after the bodies had been found, a phone call was placed from the phone booth inside the Southern Pacific train depot in Medford. A man who said his name was J. D. Harney and lived in Medford, spoke with Phyliss Haas, who was a telephone operator for Pacific Telephone and Telegraph. The man requested to be connected to the garage in Fort Klamath. He told Phyliss it was "the only one" in the area. Phyliss tried to get a clear line to place the call but all of the lines were in use.

At 1:30 p.m., when she did have a clear line, she called J. D. back. It took a few more minutes, but at 1:45 p.m., she connected J. D. with Myrtle Wimer, whose husband owned the Fort Klamath Garage. J. D. informed Myrtle that Albert had been taken ill and was in the hospital. He asked her to go to the south end of Annie Creek Canyon and pick up Albert's car. He asked that they store the car at their garage until Albert was released from the hospital. J. D. told Myrtle that the keys were in the car. Myrtle assured J. D. that she would take care of everything.

What she did not tell him was that she was going to call the police immediately because the story he told seemed very strange. Myrtle contacted the Medford Police Department. Upon hearing about her conversation with J. D., Lieutenant Charles Champlin and Sergeant Lyle Perkins rushed to the train depot, which was less than two blocks away. It was too late; there was no one near the phone booth. The police spoke with a baggage maintenance man, Al Yoakum, who informed the police that he had noticed a man in the telephone booth. Al explained to the police that he had noticed the man because he had spent so much time waiting for his call to go through. He described the man as about 5 feet 7 inches tall, between the ages of twenty-eight and thirty-five. He told the police that the man had a slender build, weighed approximately 160 pounds, and had sandy hair with a receding hairline. Lieutenant Champlin and Sergeant Perkins asked the telephone company to respond to the train depot. Upon their arrival, they dismantled the telephone from the phone booth. The police turned the telephone over to the F.B.I. They were able to obtain two prints, but they were never linked to a person.

For those visiting Crater Lake National Park that weekend, word of a double homicide spread rapidly. People were fearful and anxious to leave the area. Newspapers across the country carried the news of two executives shot execution style in Crater Lake National Park. Everyone wondered how this could possibly have happened. Those responsible for solving the crime were wondering the same thing but there were no easy answers.

The bodies were taken to Klamath Falls that evening where autopsies were performed by Klamath County Coroner Melvin George Adler. It was the belief of the coroner that the men had been killed before 4 p.m. on Saturday. The autopsy revealed that Albert had been beaten before he was shot. It did not appear that Charles had been beaten. Charles' boss, Ira Kennedy, made arrangements for Charles's body to be returned to Detroit. Albert's wife, Betty Mae, arrived in Klamath Falls to make arrangements for her husband's body.

The F.B.I. narrowed the weapon used to a foreign-made gun. The shell casings located near the bodies indicated the murder weapon had been a .32 automatic pistol. The F.B.I. believed that the murder weapon had been a 7.65-mm caliber automatic pistol. Their list of possible murder weapons included a German Mauser, Spanish Regina, Republic, or an Astra make. They told law enforcement agencies that the murder weapon could have been something else but these were the most probable brands. The F.B.I. issued a hold order throughout the country. The hold order meant that any law enforcement agency that came in contact with a subject in possession of a foreign-made gun was to detain that person for questioning.

That is exactly what happened to Ross Dallacher, age twenty-one of Richmond, California, and his friend, Ray Shankin, age twenty-two, of Rockaway Beach, California. They were stopped for speeding in Millbrae, California. They were in possession of a foreign-made gun, along with burglary tools, five knives, and $245. The men confessed to some burglaries in the California Bay Area but denied having anything to do with the Crater Lake National Park murders. Their weapon was sent to a crime lab in Washington to determine if it was the murder weapon. The ballistics test showed that it was not the weapon that killed Charles and Albert.

Ross and Ray were just two of the hundreds of people questioned by the F.B.I. They began by questioning the employees working at Crater Lake National Park; this did not turn up any viable leads. They also questioned people who were visiting Crater Lake National Park at the time of the murders.

Mr. and Mrs. Harry Cole told the investigator that they had been camping at Annie Springs on Saturday. They said they had seen two "dirty unkempt men" in a late model car in the vicinity of the murder. They went on to say that they heard two gunshots sometime in the afternoon. They remembered thinking that it was against the rules to fire a weapon in the park.

Albert's daughter, Virginia, told the authorities that she had received a letter from her father weeks before his death. In the letter he wrote in part, "things are so bad now they could not get worse." The F.B.I. was not able to decipher what Albert meant in the letter. His daughter did not have any explanation.

In Duchesne, Utah, a young hitchhiker was being questioned by the local police for his role in the Crater Lake National Park murders. A truck driver had agreed to give the hitchhiker, William K. Russell, a ride, only to become the victim of a robbery. William bragged to the truck driver that he had just murdered two men at Crater Lake National Park. He was no longer bragging when the police arrived. He was quoted as saying, "I didn't have anything to do with it. I didn't get there until Monday and they were killed on Sunday." William was not considered a viable suspect.

The F.B.I. examined 180 foreign-made automatic pistols similar to the murder weapon used to kill Charles and Albert. They checked the license plate numbers of the 537 vehicles that visited the park at the time of the murders. Referring to the undershirt used to gag the men that they thought belonged to Charles, Special Agent Joseph Santoiana told reporters that "He apparently was forced to remove it, although his outer shirt was in good order when the bodies were found."

There were thousands of leads, but each one ended up being a dead end. Weeks turned into months, months turned into years, and years turned into decades, but still the murders remain unsolved.

3

The George Dunkin Case

The name George Baker Dunkin was mentioned many times as a suspect in the Crater Lake National Park murders. While the F.B.I. was at Crater Lake National Park interviewing witnesses, the Oregon State Police was combing the nearby woods for George, who they believed killed one of their own, Phil Lowd. An armed posse of approximately twenty men from the Oregon State Police, the Jackson County Sheriff's Office, and the United States Forest Service were determined to find George and bring him in for questioning.

On June 24, 1952, Lowell Ash was working in the Persist area. Lowell was the district assistant ranger at Union Creek. Lowell heard shots and believed that someone had fired a weapon at the forest service crew that was working in the Persist area. Phil was sent to assist Lowell. Phil was familiar with George from a previous encounter. Phil had arrested George the previous year for illegally possessing deer meat. At approximately 3 p.m., Phil and Lowell approached a cabin near Buzzard Mine Road. Suddenly, one or more shots were fired. They immediately took cover behind a large log. Phil radioed for additional help. Oregon State Police Officer Charles Offenbacher responded to the scene, and he and Phil began to approach the cabin. They saw George slip out the door and disappear into the heavily wooded forest. Minutes later, additional shots rang out, and Phil fell to the ground with a gunshot to his temple.

Police were called from Medford, Roseburg, and Klamath Falls to assist. Jackson County Sheriff Howard Gault arrived on scene with several of his deputies. Other law enforcement officers were put on standby to relieve the first crew in the event that George was not located that night.

The community mourned the loss of Officer Phil Lowd. Phil was born on October 27, 1898, in North Adams, Massachusetts. He served aboard the USS *Arkansas* in the navy during World War I. In 1933, he married Claulia Klum. He had worked as a state forest patrol warden and had also been a service station operator. He served as chief deputy for Sheriff Gordon Schermerhorn. In 1932, Phil was a candidate for the Republican nomination for Jackson County Sheriff. He joined the Oregon State Police in 1932 and had been stationed in Coos and Curry counties working in game law. He also worked in Klamath Falls, Lakeview, and Medford during his twenty-year career with the Oregon State Police.

The grand jury indicted George for the murder of Officer Phil Lowd. This cleared one legal hurdle, making it possible to charge George with murder upon his capture.

George was described as being sixty-seven years old, gray hair, blue eyes, 5 feet 6 inches, and approximately 140 pounds.

Two days after Phil was murdered, Captain Paul Parson of the Oregon State Police told reporters that officers were working in groups of two in the forested area, burning empty shacks and lean-tos that could provide shelter for George. The officers knew that George would shoot anyone that he saw. Captain Parson said, "If he is cornered, it will be bad if he has any ammunition left. He has nothing to lose."

Officers left the town of Roseburg and headed to the Tiller area in case George headed in that direction. They knew George had previously walked from his cabin to Tiller overnight—approximately 30 miles by trails that the police described as "only he knows." They thought he might head to Tiller because there were fewer people in that area and he was not well-known there.

Towards the end of July, the Oregon State Police sent five officers along with a K-9 unit that belonged to the United States Army to search for George over a three-day stretch. Captain Paul Parson with the Oregon State Police explained to reporters that the five officers combed a large stretch of northern Jackson County, but they came up empty-handed. He said he believed that George was still within the 100 sq. mile area, but the rugged terrain was hampering their efforts to locate him. Captain Parson explained that George had lived in the woods his entire life and knew them well.

The authorities were contacted by George's nephew, Wes Miller. He reported that George had been to his cabin and he had given George some food and ammunition. Officers set up by Wes' cabin but were not successful at capturing him. Deputies believed George was watching them from a distance.

Fearing that they were essentially looking for a needle in a haystack, the Oregon State Police decided to fight fire with fire. They sent their best woodsmen, Officer Russell E. Maw, into the woods to live as a mountain man just like George was doing. Officer Maw reported for duty high up in the hills on August 26, 1952. He was given an alias of Jones and a fictious occupation of a trapper. He wore ankle moccasins, denim jeans, and a buckskin jacket. He sported a thin beard.

On October 18, 1952, one of the longest manhunts in Oregon's history came to a close when Officer Maw took George into custody at 7:30 a.m. Oregon State Police Captain Parson and Lieutenant Paul Morgan, along with District Attorney Paul Haviland, questioned George for two hours. George admitted that he owned a 30-30 rifle, but denied shooting anyone. He did say he fired a shot in Phil's direction, but that was just to scare him away. George was booked into the county jail. Officer Maw headed home for the first time in weeks. He told reporters he was mainly looking forward to a hot bath, something he had not had during the manhunt.

When reporters asked Officer Maw about the experience he said, "He's one of the best woodsmen I've ever seen." He went on to say, "The only difference between Dunkin and me during the last three weeks was I had a sleeping bag and he didn't have nothing."

Officer Maw told reporter Stephen A. Stone about the manhunt:

I was lucky. I was lucky in a lot of ways. I was lucky to capture George Dunkin and bring him alive out of Jackson County mountains. I was lucky to get out alive myself, for twice he drew a bead on me, and didn't shoot because his ammunition was getting low. That was before I ever saw him. He told me about it after the arrest. I was in those hills alone most of the time and followed miles of trails over mountains and through the canyons, living on cold flapjacks and bear meat. But don't think I didn't have help. I went out as special state policeman, and kept a contact with the State Police. They cooperated a thousand percent. If I wanted anything, I got it. They tell me it was the longest manhunt in Oregon since the Tracy-Merrill break from the penitentiary in 1902. There's nothing remarkable about my part in it as a one-man job, because in those mountains 500 men couldn't have done any more than one man.

When I took the job, I was told that I had a fifty-fifty chance of coming out alive. I was told that there was hardly one chance in a hundred that I could get Dunkin alive. Like I say, I was lucky. On last June 24 Dunkin killed State Police Officer Phil Lowd on Swanson Creek, fifty miles north of Medford when Lowd went to arrest him for threatening trail blazers of the forestry service. The hunt went along for weeks. On July 11 Gene Halley, ex-deputy warden of the penitentiary, suggested to Fod Malson, superintendent of the state police, that I be sent into the mountains. I've had some experience as a trailer and have hunted in southern Oregon.

So, I got a leave of absence from my job as a guard at the penitentiary. On August 25 I drove to Gold Hill and met Captain Paul Parson of the State Police, who gave me a map and a description of the area where Dunkin was thought to be hiding. The next day I drove to Trail and met Officer Fredericks of Medford, also of the State Police. He took me to the lookout station on Burnt Peak and from the tower he gave me a general view of the county. Then he took me to the place where Lowd was killed on Swanson Creek. From there we went back to the Ash homestead where Fredericks thought was a good place for a base camp.

By 2:30 that afternoon I had set up camp; a two-man war surplus nylon tent and a sleeping bag. In addition, I had only a waterproof blanket, wool on one side, and nylon on the other, that I used on the trail.

That night I made 104 flapjacks, using plenty of cornmeal. While I was doing that, my dog got uneasy, and pretty soon I shot a young bear. I cooled out the meat and the next morning fried up one hind quarter.

About seven o'clock the morning of August 27 I set out for Brush Creek, and spent the next four days in an area of about 12 square miles. Up to this time, the natives and the loggers figured that Dunkin was dead or had left there. By the afternoon of August 28, I knew definitely that he was alive in that area. So, I trailed him and found six places where he'd camped. He used his head about camping. He always built his fire on a creek bank and against a moss-covered log. He would peel the heavy moss from a log, tent it over the fire and keep it damp, and when the smoke had passed through the moss it was so filtered that you couldn't see it from fifty yards away. He was living on venison and bear, and I found several places where he had jerked the meat.

The night of August 30 I trailed Dunkin to his own cabin on Swanson Creek. He didn't hang around long, but went over into the Bitterlick country, which was on lower ground. His cabin was on a location with an elevation of 4,082 feet and Bitterlick is 2,750 feet.

Dunkin avoided trails until he got about 2,000 feet from the top of Bitterlick ridge. I knew he was in there, so I walked back to the Ash homestead, got my Jeep and drove to Trail and called Captain Parson. I told him Dunkin was very much alive and in the Bitterlick country. I asked the captain if it would be all right to move my base camp from the Ash homestead to the old Alsarena Buzzard mine, about a mile south of Dunkin's cabin where Lowd was killed. He told me to go ahead.

I didn't use the cabin at the Alsarena mine except for cooking, but slept out on the hillside. At 4 a.m. September 1 I left the Alsarena camp and went back to the Bitterlick country, and I was there September 1, 2, and 3. The night of September 3 I trailed Dunkin by his footprints out of Bitterlick as he went back to Swanson Creek.

On September 4, I investigated five old mine tunnels on Swanson Creek about half a mile below Dunkin's old cabin. The next day I trailed him to Larson's place, which had been abandoned, possibly because Dunkin had made threats against the lives of people in the district. At the Larson place he had broken a window with a shovel and stolen several cans of fruit. From Larson's he went south into the Brush Creek area again. After the arrest he admitted taking the fruit. The following day I lost track of Dunkin in the Brush Creek country, and soon realized the reason for this was that he had doubled back to Swanson Creek area and then back into the Bitterlick. He'd shot a beaver and eaten all of it but the entrails, hide, and toenails. He told me that later.

I was in the Bitterlick all night of September 8. He pulled out of there the morning of the 9th because it was snowing and getting colder. I trailed him south to the Alder Creek area. Then I walked back to the mine, got the Jeep and drove to the Art Moore ranch. I picked up Dunkin's trail at Alder Creek and followed him to Persist the morning of the 10th. He was about half way between Persist and the ranch of Wes Miller, who is Dunkin's nephew.

That was the first time I saw George Dunkin. He was about 2,000 yards away, going south through an opening in the timber. I went back to the Moore ranch and contacted a man named Ted Shemick. I don't know how you spell that name, but that's the way it sounded. I asked him where Miller's ranch was, and he told me Miller would be at the Moore place about noon. It was then a quarter of eleven. About noon Miller drove up in his Jeep. He called Shemick to the barn. "We've got to go down to the Hanson place where they have a radio, Miller told him, "and notify the State Police at Medford that George Dunkin has been at my place this afternoon. "We won't have to do that," Shemick told him. "There's a State Police officer here now."

They came into the house and Miller told me that Dunkin had been at his place and wanted food, matches, shoes, and overalls. Miller said he had given him two pounds of beans, a slab of bacon, loaf of bread, overalls and a shirt, and had asked Miller to get him a box of 30-30 cartridges.

Miller had told him he would get the shells, but warned him that the State Police were watching him awful close. Then, Miller said, the old man wanted to trade his 30-30 for Miller's 25-20 rifle. Miller told him he couldn't do that, because the police knew what kind of guns he had. Miller told him he would get the shells and leave them in a grain bin in the barn.

I drove to Rogue Elk and called Captain Parson, and had him send me a box of .32 specials and a box of 30-30s. I put the 32s in a 30-30 box and put the box in the grain bin. I did that because I knew he would come back, and in case I slipped up somewhere he wouldn't be able to shoot anyone with 32s in a 30-30 rifle.

I started laying in on those shells the morning of September 11, staying in the house at the Wes Miller place 24 hours a day until September 18 when the arrest was made. On the 18th he came to the ranch after the shells and Miller told him they were at the house, because the State Police were watching the barn. "Well, we'll go to the house and get them," Dunkin answered. As he stepped to the door I had him covered with my rifle. "Mr. Dunkin," I said, "you're under arrest for the murder of Phil Lowd." He was standing there with his rifle sagging along his leg. "Who are you?" he asked. "Are you a State Police officer?" "Yes, I am," I told him.

He handed his gun to his nephew, and still covering him, I handcuffed him. He carried an old case knife and an old pack sack. On the way to Medford, he told me that he'd had two chances to shoot me after he decided I was an officer, and would have done it if he'd had more ammunition. One of those times was in Bitterlick Canyon. The other was one night at the Alsarena mine when I sat in the cabin behind a kerosene lamp writing a letter. That time I was warned by my dog. I was scared, but all I could do was pretend not to be and just keep on writing.[1]

Special District Attorney Paul Haviland originally charged George with first-degree murder. After conferring with the Oregon State Police, he dropped the charge down to second-degree murder. There was concern that they would not be able to obtain a conviction of murder in the first degree.

George's brother, sister, and two nephews traveled from Southern California to see him. They spoke at length about the trial and the plea. They convinced George to take a plea. George's attorney, Edward Kelly, told the reporters that George had been ill for some time and did not feel up to a prolonged trial.

Early on the morning of September 26, 1952, George appeared before Circuit Judge H. K. Hanna. He was dressed in a blue work shirt and gray pants. He appeared to be quite nervous. Judge Hanna asked George how he pled, to which George replied, "To second-degree murder?" When Judge Hanna told him that the charge was second-degree murder, George said, "I plead guilty to second-degree murder." With that, he was sentenced to life imprisonment.

When reporters stopped by the county jail to talk with George, they found him sitting in the hallway, smoking cigarettes. He was in his stocking feet, awaiting new shoes to replace the ones he had worn during his time in the mountains.

When asked about the case, George claimed that he did not shoot Phil intentionally and that he did not know that he had actually shot Phil until a month after the occurrence. He continually referred to the murder as "the accident." He did say it was "something a man could never forget, no matter how long he lives." He told the reporters that he had received "fine treatment" at the county jail and hoped that the same would be true in prison. George did have concerns that there would be enough to eat in prison. Recovering from his almost three months in the wild, he explained that he did not realize that hunger "could hang on as it has." He said he had had "plenty of grub" in the county jail, but it still was not enough to satisfy his hunger. He also spoke of his hopes of receiving dentures to replace his three teeth and to receive medical care at the state prison. George was also looking forward to being around people after having lived for many years as a recluse. He told the reporters, "I'll have someone to talk to, and they tell me there are moving pictures once a week." George explained, "It's not good for a man to be all by himself with nothing to do."

George spoke freely to the reporters about the day Phil was murdered. He said that the officers fired "about twenty shots and I thought they were shooting at me." He "was mad and scared." He said, "I grabbed my rifle, ran out of their line of vision, and shot in the direction from which they had been shooting." He recalled only shooting once; Oregon State Police proved that he shot twice. He did admit that "after thinking it over," he realized that the shots fired by the officers were not aimed at him.

George told the reporters that he ran from his cabin only wearing, "a pair of worn-out slippers and no socks." He had his rifle and seven shells. He told of how he suffered a deep cut to his ankle, then said, "but I treated it with balsam and it didn't get infected." He admitted that he returned to his cabin the next morning and grabbed a pair of mackinaw shoes, some salt pork, flour, sugar, and a frying pan but that he was "so excited" that he forgot to take a knife.

The food he took only lasted ten days. There was some flour and sugar left that he mixed with water and ate. George recalled that one day he came across some stock salt on a log. He said, "it wasn't meant for humans but it sure tasted good." He said when his food supply ran out, he lived on nuts that he found in the forest. He boasted that one day, "I came face to face with a bear and luckily it only took one shot to kill it." George told the reporters that he dragged and rolled the bear back to his camp and proceeded to cook the meat.

George denied ever sitting in ambush for law enforcement. He referred to Maw's statement as a "pipe dream." He did admit to knowing that the police were trying to keep him from obtaining anymore ammunition. He believed that was for fear that, "I would go hog wild and kill everybody, but I only wanted ammunition so I could get meat."

When asked about his arrest, George said, "I thought it was a joke when Maw told me I was under arrest." He explained that Maw did not look like a police officer, "but I knew it wasn't a joke when he got out his handcuffs." He claimed he stopped by his nephew's cabin on three occasions and it was his nephew who told him he had killed Officer Phil Lowd. When his nephew begged him to turn himself in, he said it was fear that kept him from doing so. George elaborated saying, "I knew I was considered a maniac after Wes told me of the killing. I didn't know but what they'd lynch me, or beat me to death."

Towards the end of the interview, George told the reporters, "I'm glad it's all over. It was getting mighty cold up there." When the interview was over, George said in an obvious understatement, "Don't worry about taking up my time. I've got nothing but time from now on."

4

Dupree Poe

Larry Austin was awoken at 2:35 a.m. on May 2, 1931, to the sound of a gunshot and breaking glass. He immediately went to his window and saw a dark-green 1928 Chevrolet Coach with disc wheels speeding away. Larry lived in an apartment above the Club Pool Hall in Silverton. He ran downstairs and saw a body lying in front of the Pool Hall. Night police officer Hans James Iverson, age fifty-six, had been shot to death. Larry contacted the local police and they arrived moments later.

Mayor C. Eastman put out an alarm to law enforcement agencies in Portland, Salem, Eugene, Woodburn, and Molalla to be on the lookout for the vehicle described by the witness. By 4 a.m., all of Willamette Valley was being patrolled in search of the suspect car. In addition to the patrols, officers began arriving from the outlying areas to assist.

Officer Iverson was born in Iowa. He worked as a deputy sheriff in Iowa. He arrived in Silverton in 1919. He worked at the Silver Falls Mill. He had worked as a night police officer for two years. He and his wife had a son and a daughter. Their son, D. N., lived in Portland, and was employed driving a truck between Portland and Silverton. Their daughter, Marie, worked at a hardware store in Silverton.

Officer Iverson was found lying on his back. He had been shot through the back of his head. His hand was resting on his revolver. The safety lock had not been removed. The position of the body indicated he was looking into the pool room when he was shot. The police investigating the crime scene did not find any spent cartridges. They believed that revenge could have been the motive.

The citizens of Silverton woke to the shocking news that a police officer had been killed in the line of duty. It was the first murder in Silverton in forty years.

Lieutenant J. J. Keegan, Officer A. B. Chase, and Officer M. A. McMeeken of the Portland Police Department arrived in Silverton to assist with the investigation. They were told that the Club Pool Hall had been robbed two weeks prior. Officer Iverson had arrested two juveniles for the crime. Lieutenant Keegan speculated that Officer Iverson heard something or someone in the pool hall and was looking in the window when he was shot.

Within hours, L. E. Darkins and Lawrence Reid were brought to the police station for questioning. They had been released from the Marion County jail days before. After questioning, the police were satisfied that they had no knowledge of the murder of Officer Iverson and they were free to go.

The authorities soon learned that a car matching the description of the one speeding away from the pool hall had been reported stolen the evening of the murder. Mr. and Mrs. E. R. Sims from Medford were in Silverton visiting Harry Sims when their car was stolen. The Sims' car was located abandoned in The Dalles. They were able to lift fingerprints from the vehicle and send the prints to the Portland Police Department to see if there was a match.

On May 4, 1931, services were held for Officer Iverson. All businesses in town closed for two hours during the time of the service. Reverend Thomas Hardie and Melvin W. S. Gordon officiated the service. The crowd in the church was so large that it spilled out into the street.

State Traffic Patrol Officer P. E. Clayton brought two brothers in for questioning. Lester and S. E. Irvingham were arrested and held for investigation. A service station attendant had noticed their car had tire treads similar to the marks made by the car that sped from the scene of the crime. Police located two guns in the car. Upon questioning, the brothers told conflicting stories as to when the guns had last been fired. Deputy District Attorney Lyle Page went to The Dalles to compare their fingerprints to those on the Sims' car. When their fingerprints failed to match those on the Sims' car, they were released.

The police were frustrated as the weeks turned into months, and there were still no suspects in the crime. Finally, seven months after the crime, Mayor Eastman was told that they knew someone who would be willing to talk if the reward was increased.

Paul Krier had told some friends in Silverton that when the reward was increased, he would tell the police who was responsible. Deputy

Sheriff Burkhart and Oregon State Police Sergeant Dodele questioned Paul, who initially denied ever saying anything relating to the case. When confronted with the fact that his friends had already told Mayor Eastman, he admitted that he did have information. He immediately named Robert Ripley. Paul said Robert was serving time somewhere in Washington state. The investigators packed their bags and headed to Washington State Reformatory at Monroe where Robert was serving one to ten years for stealing chickens.

Robert confessed to Oregon State Police Sergeant Dodele and Deputy Sheriff Sam Burkhart that he was involved in the murder of Officer Iverson. He implicated Paul Krier and Richard Hyland in the crime. They adamantly denied having any involvement. Robert later admitted he had lied when he named them. Paul and Richard were held for other crimes but not for the murder of Officer Iverson. Robert also named Frank Manning, age twenty-six. Officers learned that Frank was on a steamship heading for Asia.

The one person who Robert named, but they couldn't locate, was Dupree "Buck" Poe, age thirty-two. Hundreds of flyers were printed and mailed to law enforcement agencies across the country. Dupree's sister's house in Texas was put under surveillance in case he showed up there. In Robert's confession, he said Dupree was the one who fired the gun and killed Officer Iverson. About the only thing Robert was able to tell the police about Dupree was that he was a drug addict, he used to work as a seaman, and was last known to be in the Portland area.

In Robert's signed confession, he stated that Frank and Dupree were with him in Portland. They decided to take a Milwaukee street car. From there they took a train to Salem. They got off the train and walked for an unknown amount of time. They spotted the Sims' car on a street and immediately decided to steal it. He recalled they drove through Silverton and then out onto Silver Falls Road for 4 or 5 miles. They parked and stayed there until approximately 2:15 a.m. Next, they drove back into Silverton where they parked in front of the Club Pool Hall. Robert described the next minutes:

> Frank got out and was walking over to the door of the pool hall when the officer was spotted coming across the street. When the officer was about ten feet or so from the car, Dupree ordered him to throw them up. The officer apparently dived into his clothing after a gun. The officer turned to face Frank, who was standing against the fender of the car, when Dupree fired. We then drove for the Old Silverton Highway going towards Salem.[1]

Robert told the investigators that either Frank or Dupree threw the 25–35 caliber rifle and a satchel into a lake. He said they drove to The Dalles where they abandoned the car. They walked into The Dalles and caught a train to Spokane. When the train pulled into Spokane, they parted ways. He said that he went to Seattle, then Portland before going to his father's house in Chemawa. Robert admitted that the three of them planned to break into the Club Pool Hall and blow open the safe.

The police were waiting for Frank to return home from Asia. Upon his arrival, they were there to arrest him for his part in the murder of Officer Iverson. Frank was offered a chance to testify against Robert and Dupree in the hopes of receiving a lesser sentence.

Finding the third man, Dupree, was not proving to be easy. The local police sent inquiries to law enforcement agencies in America and to foreign countries as well. The director of criminology service, French Republic, replied to the flyer they received. The letter was written in their native language but when translated read:

> [From] Repubique Hellenique Minister of Interior, Director of Criminologie service, June 3, 1932.
> [To] Bureau of Investigation, Salem, Oregon.
> Mr. Director: In response to your letter of the 26th, I have the honor of informing you that in our collection we have not found fingerprints corresponding to those which you sent us, and belonging to one named Dupree Poe or Dupree Buck sought by you for various motives.
> The name mentioned does not appear in our alphabetical collection either.
> Please let me know, in due time, the result of the action eventually taken by you against the suspect.
> Please have the assurance, Mr. Director, of my highest consideration.
> By order of the Minister, The Director, Garduy.[2]

Meanwhile, up north in Seattle, a man by the name of Paul King was arrested for stealing an electric drill. Detective Dick Mahoney thought he recognized something in King. A bit more digging and it was discovered that King and Poe shared the same tattoos. On his left arm, he had a tattoo of a rose. On his right arm, he had a tattoo of a cowgirl and a cat. Confronted with this information, King admitted that he was, in fact, Dupree Poe.

Dupree waived extradition and was soon in the company of Deputy Sheriff Burkhart and State Police Officer Dodele. They returned to Salem, and Dupree was placed in the Marion County jail.

On July 19, 1932, twelve jurors were selected to hear the evidence against Dupree. The jury consisted of seven woman and five men. The jurors included Merle Ramp, Edna Williams, Lena Grabenhorst, Richard Harrison, Rose Cole, Pearl Kinzer, Georgia Shearer, C. D. Oppen, Jesse Crabb, Edward Bengs, E. S. Coates, and D. L. Shrode. Judge Fred Wilson presided over the trial. District Attorney John Carson and Deputy District Attorney Page asked for the death penalty. Dupree was represented by Paul Burris, Francis Fuller, and Philmore Huth.

Frank turned state's evidence and was called to the stand. He told the court that he had been a casual acquaintance of Robert and Dupree. They had convinced him they knew of "an easy job," that being a robbery of the Club Pool Hall in Silverton. The three prepared nitroglycerine explosives at Robert's family farm. Robert had two guns in his possession at the farm. Frank stated they arrived in Silverton at 2 a.m. They spotted Officer Iverson and asked him for directions to a garage. As he approached the car, he was ordered to surrender. As he reached for his gun, Dupree shot him from the back seat. Frank said they fled the scene of the crime. He said that when they were driving over a bridge near Champoeg, they tossed the guns into the water. After that, they went to The Dalles.

Dupree took the stand and declared that he had nothing to do with the actual shooting. He told the jury that he was not with Frank and Robert at the time of the murder. He claimed that they had dropped him off at the Robert's family ranch and he did not know where they went.

Oregon State Police Sergeant Dodele and Deputy Sheriff Burkhart both testified as to what Robert had told them in his confession.

On July 28, 1932, the jury returned a verdict of guilty in the first degree. Dupree was sentenced to life imprisonment. The only thing he said to the court was that he bore no ill feelings.

A jury was impaneled for Robert's trial. The jury went on a tour of the house where the Sims' car had been stolen, to the crime scene, and to Robert's family farm. In his opening statements, Robert's attorney, Chris Kowitz, stated he would show that Robert had nothing to do with the murder and had not taken any steps to prepare for a burglary. Officer Iverson's wife testified, as did Mayor Eastman, Chief of Police Henry Storli, Sheriff Bower, Deputy Sheriff Burkhart, and Larry Austin. The trial had barely gotten underway when Robert withdrew his plea of not guilty and pled guilty to murder in the first degree. Judge Wilson sentenced Robert to life imprisonment.

Frank was convicted of manslaughter. He was sentenced to ten years in prison for his role in the death of Officer Iverson. The court held that he was equally guilty for planning the burglary but that he did not intend to kill Officer Iverson. Judge Wilson advised the state prison officials to keep Frank away from Dupree and Robert.

The year 1933 saw the first of many of Dupree's attempts to escape from prison. He managed to work loose a sewage pipe connection that he planned to use to spring the lock on his cell door. Warden Lewis explained that even if he had successfully gotten out of his cell, he still would have been in the main building.

There was general unrest among the prisoners in 1936. They had been saying for weeks that they would riot if fellow prisoner Roy La Nair lost his bid for release from prison. Judge Arlie Walker denied the request. That afternoon, the inmates working in the kitchen announced they were going on strike and would not prepare anymore meals until the parole system was changed. Frank Tilson, who was serving five years for burglary, got eighty prisoners together in the yard. They in turn released hundreds of prisoners. They raided the commissary and brought a huge quantity of food and cigarettes into the prison yard. The rioters went to Dupree's solitary cell and set him free. The rioters took tools from the machine shop and drugs from the hospital. By this time, there were an estimated 700 prisoners in the prison yard. Oregon State Police sent officers from McMinnville, Oregon City, Portland, and Salem to assist. Just before the extra reinforcements arrived, some of the men made a run for the wall and shots rang out. One inmate was killed and two were wounded. As order was restored, prison officials realized Dupree was missing. He was later found along with another inmate from the solitary block, Theodore Jordan.

On the night of Halloween 1951, twenty prisoners overpowered seven prison guards with knives and a gun. The prisoners were heading back to their cells after dinner when they overpowered the guards and pushed them into cells. They then released 380 prisoners from their cells. Next, the prisoners crossed over a construction area in the front of the prison and were about to reach the turnkey gates and head out the front entrance when they heard a voice. Prison guard Maurice Folquet saw the twenty escapees from a catwalk on the other side of the construction area. He was not aware of the escape attempt; he was simply returning from his dinner and saw them. He yelled at them to return to their cells. Surprisingly, they did just that.

By the time they returned, 380 prisoners had been left unguarded for thirty minutes. Among the twenty escapees was Dupree. He was one of the instigators who created a diversion so the prisoners could overpower the guards. Even though the prisoners returned to their cells, the Oregon State Police stood by in case there was more trouble. They were released from their duties when it was determined that everything was calm. Later, Allen Brumfield told the prison officials that no one had forced him to go along with the escape. He said, "I got on the little red wagon all by myself. I grabbed hold of a train that I thought was leaving." He said when the train derailed, he returned. Dupree was more concerned about the culinary choices in the isolation cell that he was headed to. He asked if he would be subjected to the "California Dog Biscuit," prison lingo for a tasteless meal served to those in isolation. When asked what his plea was for the escape attempt, Dupree replied, "A prison is no place to be pleading guilty to anything." With that, he pled innocent. Nevertheless, Dupree and all of the escapees were placed in isolation for thirty days for their role in the escape attempt.

An investigation revealed that a prison guard, Francis McConnell, age twenty-seven, was responsible for smuggling the gun and knives into the prison for the Halloween escape attempt. *The Capital Journal* reported:

> The case against McConnell was built up after he outlined details in a statement to state police. On the surface, it was another case of the smooth-talking artistry of Dupree Poe, a lifer sentenced for killing Constable Iverson of Silverton 20 years ago, combined with the guard's need for money.[3]

Francis told Oregon State Police Captain Ray Howard and Lieutenant Farley Mogan that he became familiar with Dupree when he was placed in an isolation cell that he was in charge of. Dupree asked him if he wanted to make some money, and "the idea struck home."

Dupree concocted a plan wherein Francis would smuggle dynamite and guns into the prison. Dupree and his inmate friends, John Omar Pinson and William Benson, would escape. The three of them would go to Portland and rob a store. They would pass 25 percent of the robbery proceeds to Francis' mother-in-law, who, in turn, would pass the proceeds to him.

Francis went ahead and got five sticks of dynamite. He had previously loaned his .22 caliber revolver to a friend but he retrieved that. He slipped the contraband to Dupree. Prison Guard Captain Roy Riggs discovered the dynamite and the weapon in the bed of another prisoner, John Ralph. Francis became an inmate himself, charged with aiding an attempt to escape, leaving his eighteen-year-old wife and one-month-old baby at home.

This was not the only time Dupree made friends with a prison employee. Frederick Beck, a school supervisor at the prison, found himself on the wrong side of the law after helping Dupree. The case began after William Berry was sent to prison for statutory rape involving his fourteen-year-old daughter. His wife, Grace, sold some of his logging equipment to cover her living expenses. She was left to raise five children and run a 160-acre ranch in Reedsport after William went to prison. William asked her to send $4,000 to Dupree Poe at a Salem address. He assured her the money would be used to get him out of prison. The address Grace sent the money to was the home of Frederick Beck. Oregon State Police Lieutenant Farley Morgan arrested Frederick when he signed for the registered letter. Grace told the authorities she had no idea that Dupree was an inmate or that there was anything against the law in sending the money.

A jury was selected for Frederick's case. Frederick pled innocent to the charge of grand larceny. He posted $3,500 bail and was released from the county jail. When the trial began, details emerged that Frederick was to receive 10 percent of the money mailed to Dupree. Testimony also revealed that Frederick was implicated in smuggling five Benzedrine inhalers into the prison. The jury deliberated for six hours before returning with a verdict of not guilty.

Dupree never gave up on escaping from the walls that held him in prison. One time, he was able to walk out of prison wearing "dress out" clothing. He had managed to set aside a change of clothing that inmates are given upon their release from prison. He changed into the clothing and walked out the front door of the prison along with some visitors. Warden George Alexander spotted him before he could make it out of the prison yard.

Early on the morning of October 28, 1952, Prison Guard Sergeant Carl Watson saw an inmate running through the segregation unit. It turned out that six inmates had somehow sprung their locks and were running towards the shower room. They quickly sawed through a bar in the shower room window and tore the heavy mesh screen off. Carl and five other guards ran outside only to be grabbed by the six escapees. They had a knife and told the guards "We're taking over." The inmates forced the guards to go with them as they made their way across the prison yard through the thick fog. The escapees attempted to scale a wall with a makeshift ladder that was hidden among some construction materials.

Armed guards were waiting for them at the top of the wall. The prison had implemented a "fog line" for just such occasions. Fearing that the guards would not be able to spot escapees, they added a shift on foggy nights to guard the wall. When they were unable to get over the wall, they found a box car on a spur track. They still had hold of the six guards. They unlocked a derailing switch and pried the wheels just enough to get the boxcar moving. They forced the guards to lie in a trench beside the spur. The boxcar began moving but picked up speed and ended up crashing into a prison gate. The guards from the wall opened fire and within moments other guards arrived and took possession of the escapees. Two of the six escapees were slightly wounded, but Dupree was unscathed. All six of the guards were fine.

The following year saw Dupree once again trying to escape. Dupree and other inmates brandished homemade knives and grabbed five unarmed guards. The guards were pushed into a cell. They released more inmates, although some refused to participate and remained in their cells. Dupree and his fellow escapees demanded that Warden Virgil O'Malley extend their time in the exercise yard and give them regular sentences for time required in the segregation cell. By this time, fifty guards armed with rifles and tear gas had arrived. Warden O'Malley explained to each of the inmates serving time in solitary how long they would have to remain there. The sentences ranged from two to seven months. He assured Dupree and the others that he would consider their request for the extra time in the exercise yard. The guards were released unharmed. Guard David Kowitz later told reporters he was grabbed from behind by inmate Albert Doolin. Albert held his hair while putting a knife to his throat. He quoted inmate Albert as saying, "If you don't give us what we want, we'll cut your throat."

That same year, Dupree and two other inmates attacked a guard in the exercise yard. Guard R. Howell suffered a black eye and cuts on his head and face.

In 1956, Judge George Duncan denied Dupree's motion that demanded the state prove the validity of his incarceration. At the time, he had an appeal pending with the Oregon Supreme Court contending that he was a native of Manchuria and asked for repatriation to Manchuria. He signed legal documents swearing to the fact that he was a citizen of the Republic of China by "right and birth and choice." When he was arrested in 1932, he listed his place of birth as Mt. Vernon, Texas. In 1958, Dupree received a letter stating that his father had died and left him an interest in mineral rights in Texas.

Dupree spent the next years petitioning the circuit court, the State Supreme Court, and the Federal Court. It was not just for himself that he filed petitions; he became the self-appointed prison lawyer and filed on behalf of his fellow inmates. His request for a law library for his cell was turned down by Judge Val Sloper after he demanded that Warden Clarence Gladden and Attorney General Robert Thornton cover the $1,000 cost. Dupree referred to himself as the "shadow warden."

In 1963, Dupree was granted parole and walked out of the prison that had held him for thirty-one years. Prison officials arranged for him to work as a stock clerk in a warehouse in Washington.

5

Oregon Jones

Oregon Jones' parents were immigrants who first settled in the Midwest. They came out west and decided that Douglas County was perfect for them. They were so taken with the state of Oregon that when their son was born in 1901, they decided to name him Bert Oregon Jones. As a young man, Bert took on the name, "Oregon." Soon, Oregon Jones became more and more like the outlaws he idolized. He was still a juvenile in 1915, when he and a friend broke into a warehouse and stole several items. He was sentenced to one to seven years at the state school in Salem. This would be the beginning of a long, criminal career.

In 1922, law enforcement agencies in Josephine County became aware of some brazen highway robberies where innocent motorists were being forced to stop their cars and being robbed at gunpoint. The local police in Grants Pass had their hands full with burglaries. An investigation by the Josephine County Sheriff's Office led them to Oregon Jones and his brother, Dewey. Josephine County Sheriff Lewis and Deputy Lister raided the Jones' home on West L Street in Grants Pass and located many stolen items. The victims were asked to come to the sheriff's office to determine if any of the recovered property belonged to them. In doing so, the Jones brothers were positively identified as the highway robbers and the ones who committed the recent burglaries.

Oregon Jones made a full confession and described one of the highway robberies. He said:

The next holdup we pulled was at about five miles south of Grants Pass, on September 5, 1922, we noticed an auto camped there as there was some people around a camp fire, it was about 9 pm when we passed them in my Mitchell auto. I drove my car to Grants Pass, then we walked back, when we got there, it was raining, this was about 1 a.m. We found three men and two ladies and one small boy. We held these people up at the point of a gun, and relieved them of about $25 in money, one or two watches. I made one of the men take off a heavy wool shirt and told him every time he looked around at us, I would take some of his clothing off of him. While doing this we both wore white masks over our faces. I examined their car which was a new Maxwell, and as I found they had a full tank of gas, we made them pile in the back seat, and I drove them to the top of Sexton Mountain, about 14 miles north of Grants Pass, when we met another auto coming south, this was about 2:30 a.m. This car was owned by Radcliff, who stopped and asked us how much more bad road there was before they got to good road on the highway. I told them that we would take him over the rest of it. By this time my partner got on the other side of them. I then flashed my light on them and ordered them to hold their hands up, my partner holding a gun on them. In this car there was one man, his wife and a small boy. We relieved them of about $80 in money, one man's watch, one ladies wrist watch, one or two diamond rings, and about three suitcases of clothing. We put all the articles we wanted in the large Studebaker car, and also piled the nine people in the back seat of this car and covered them over with a blanket. I drove this car while my partner sat in the front seat with me and left them all about seven miles north of Grants Pass. After they all left the car, we left some clothing and blankets, also some matches and told them that a couple of men could walk and get the Maxwell car that we left, then they could come back and pick up the women. I also told Mr. Radcliff I would leave his car at the point where we had held up the Maxwell car. My partner and I then started with the car toward Grants Pass when we met another auto going north, they were traveling about forty miles an hour, I then turned our car around and when I passed them, I turned our car across the road and stopped them. This car was occupied by one man, one lady and small boy. We held them up at the point of a gun and relieved them of about $40 in money and two diamond rings. I pawned these diamond rings at Zemakey's Loan Office at Sacramento, California. For the man's ring I got $35 and for the ladies ring I got $230. I also hocked Mrs. Radcliff's diamond ring at this place for $35. I also sold three or four watches at this place. I believe all these articles were hocked by me under the name of Frank Burgerman and gave address as city.[1]

Oregon Jones also admitted to robbing several Southern Pacific Railway employees at Grants Pass the previous year. He admitted to several other crimes in the past occurring in Josephine County. Oregon Jones showed the deputies where he had buried some of the loot around Josephine County.

Although Oregon Jones signed a confession, he pled not guilty in court. During the Jones' brothers' trial, several victims testified. One woman even recognized Oregon Jones' distinctive voice.

Upon learning of Oregon Jones' confession, Jackson County Sheriff Terrill figured the Jones' brothers were probably responsible for a highway robbery in his county. In that case, Sprague Reigel and seven friends were heading home late at night after a dance. They were forced to stop their car. They were robbed of their possessions and left stranded after the robbers stole their vehicle. Although Oregon Jones confessed to this highway robbery, even admitting to hitting Sprague with a blackjack, he later told the court that the confession was just a "fairy tale."

The *Grants Pass Courier* reported:

The case against the Jones brothers has aroused more interest than any trial in Josephine County for years. The courtroom has been crowded daily with people who got there as soon as the doors were opened in the morning. Many took their lunch with them and remained during the noon hour so that they would not lose their seats. The case was hard fought from the start. The confession by Oregon Jones created quite a sensation in itself. People are inclined to believe that he was trying to emulate the James boys in their daring crimes. It's believed that with these men convicted that there will be a great lessening of crime in the city during the summer, as Oregon Jones laid claim to nearly every robbery committed.[2]

Oregon and Dewey Jones were booked into jail. Once in jail, the authorities learned the brothers had served time in Oklahoma for burglary. By piecing everything together, they figured out that Oregon Jones was sent to the state school in Salem in 1915 and released in 1916. The following year, Oregon and Dewey were behind bars in Oklahoma.

This time though, Oregon Jones did not stay long in jail. Within a couple of weeks, he and Ellsworth Kelly escaped from jail. When the jailer, Schroeder, went into their cell, they overpowered him, stole his gun, and fled. Dewey was housed in another cell and did not partake in the escape. A reward of $500 was offered for the capture of Oregon Jones and Ellsworth.

The escapees made it to Evanston, Wyoming, before being captured after two weeks on the run. Sheriff Lewis and Deputy Lister went to Wyoming to fetch the escapees. They returned them to Josephine County before transporting them by train to the prison in Salem. For the trip north, they placed leg irons on the prisoners. During the entire train ride, they sat with their guns at the ready.

It did not take long for the Jones' brothers, Ellsworth Kelly, and their new friends, George Hotlsclaw and George Jackson, to cook up an escape plan. While the rest of the prisoners were enjoying the Lions minstrel show, the five convicts stayed in their cells. As the orchestra played, they began sawing the bars on their cells with the saws they had stolen from the prison shop. They managed to get out of their cells and saw a hole in the roof to climb through. They made it to the prison wall before prison guards put an end to their plan. It turned out that some of their fellow inmates had notified the guards of their plan. They returned to their cells to plan their next escape.

Meanwhile, back in Jackson County, Sheriff Terrill finally located the other Jones brother that he had been looking for. He was confident that Milam was responsible for robberies in his county. He took a train to Los Angeles and brought Milam back along with a woman, Ruth Brown, who was in a relationship with Milam. Ruth had been the benefactor of many pieces of jewelry that Milam had stolen during his highway robberies. Ruth had given birth to a baby six months prior and she told Sheriff Terrill that the baby was Milam's.

Milam, Ruth, and the baby, Virginia June, settled in at the Jackson County jail. Sheriff Terrill asked Ruth if the baby's last name was Jones or Brown. She replied, "Brown, I guess."

The sheriff asked, "It must seem tough to have her in jail?"

Ruth was quick to reply, "Virginia June don't know whether she is in jail, or Japan." Although Ruth appeared quite comfortable in her new surroundings, she did fear that an agency would remove the baby from her care. Ruth was to be held as a material witness, but the officials said, "the county jail was decided as not a fit place" for her baby. She was released from custody and left for Albany to stay with relatives. As the trial got underway, other relatives of the Jones' brothers were present in the courtroom. Dewey's wife, and their son, Dewey David, Jr., were there, along with a sister of the Jones' brothers. Her husband testified that Ruth was in possession of many pieces of the stolen jewelry.

While Milam was busy with his trial, Oregon Jones was busy with his next escape plan. During broad daylight, Jones and five others broke out of the Oregon State Penitentiary. The inmates who were with Oregon Jones included Tom Murray, serving ten years for robbing a bank in Florence; William Johnson, serving five years for larceny; C. M. Weekly, serving fifteen years for robbery; Joe Johnson, waiting on his sentence for robbery; and Ellsworth Kelly, serving twenty years for his previous escape with Oregon Jones.

Once outside the prison, they came across Charles Spurlin. They hit him over the head and got in his car. They drove into the woods about 1 mile, then forced Charles out of his car and took off. Within hours, there were more than 100 men on the hunt for the six escapees. The posse came across Charles and assisted him.

Prison officials sent word of the escape to all law enforcement agencies. Many of the agencies joined the posse in an attempt to capture all six inmates before they did more harm. Citizen volunteers joined the dragnet, and soon, men were stretched all over Oregon.

The next morning, when the owner of Spier and Sons General Merchandise Store in Aumsville arrived at work, they discovered their store had been broken into. The police arrived and discovered that shotgun shells, tobacco, flashlights, knives, groceries, clothing, and shoes had been stolen. They immediately suspected the six escapees. Law enforcement fanned out and went door to door, seeking their men.

William Johnson was the first to be apprehended. His taste of freedom lasted less than forty-eight hours. He told the authorities that their plan was to head south, which they did, but they could hear sirens closing in on them. He said Oregon Jones found a side road and they abandoned the car. He said from then on, they stayed low digging through trees and brush as they went. William said they stuck together until someone spotted Deputy Warden Lilley and everyone scattered. He retold how he raised his head from the brush just to get a quick glance, and Deputy Warden Lilley began shooting his rifle. William said the shots missed his head by inches and he got away. He laid down in the brush for a few hours and then began traveling again. It was then that he ran right into the waiting arms of prison guard Lute Savage.

When asked about the escape plan, William said it had been in the works for weeks. He said they made keys for the three doors that led to the basement. There, they used a hacksaw that William had stolen from a shop, and they cut through the bars on the basement window ahead of time.

Prison officials believed they had spotted Oregon Jones as he tried to make his way into Linn County. One guard fired fourteen rounds, but if it was Oregon Jones, he got away. A citizen thought he saw two of the escapees cooking a chicken over a fire out in the woods. Other tips came in, but they did not result in an arrest.

C. M. Weekly was located near Stayton. He quietly gave up and was returned to prison. Joe Johnson also gave up when confronted by the authorities. Tom Murray was taken into custody after being spotted in some brush by M. J. Melchior and O. Olsen of the National Guard, who were looking for the escapees. Tom was with Oregon Jones who managed to get away. Tom tried to get over a fence but gave up as the shots got closer. Tom was armed with the loaded revolver he had stolen from the Doerfler house.

Ward Irvine and Jack Eakin returned him to the prison where Warden Dairymple was waiting along with several reporters. As he entered the room, he greeted the warden, who replied, "Hello, Murray, I am glad to see you back."

Tom quickly replied, "I'm not." He regaled his audience with his tales of his six-night adventure in the brush. He told how they had been fired upon by Deputy Warden Lilley within the first hours of their escape. He spoke of breaking into the Spier and Sons General Merchandise Store in Aumsville. Tom admitted that he and Oregon Jones were the men seen cooking a chicken over a fire. He said that stolen chickens were their main food source. He added that they cooked the birds over dry wood, to minimize the amount of smoke seen by the posse. Tom said the witness did not know they were escapees and offered them a job cutting wood. They politely declined the offer. Spooked by being seen, the two men moved down the road several miles before resuming cooking their chicken. He told of breaking into the Doerfler house and stealing their car. Tom said they drove to the railroad in the hopes of hopping a freight train but there were too many guards there so they left. He did say they made several attempts at crossing the Santiam River, but it was always too heavily guarded. He said when they were at the highway bridge at Jefferson, they were so close to the guards, they could hear their conversations. When Warden Dairymple asked if he would attempt another escape, Tom replied that he did not think so.

Apparently, Tom changed his mind about escaping because just four months later, he and prisoner Eugene Kidder cut through the iron bars on a grate that led to a power flume. They swam under the water through the flume. At the time, law enforcement was busy looking for two other escapees, but they did manage to capture Tom three weeks later. Eugene made it to Montana but was arrested there for larceny. He served his sentence there and was returned to Oregon five years later.

While the posse was busy searching for Oregon Jones, his brother down in Jacksonville made a decision. True to the family name, Milam escaped from the Jackson County jail before the trial was finished. He made his break when the jailer, John Robinson, entered his cell. Milam struck Robinson with his fists, taking him to the ground. He stole Robinson's gun and headed for the hills. Another inmate, Jesus Gomez, also escaped but his freedom was short lived when he was spotted by law enforcement.

Warden Dalrymple told reporters, "It is thought likely by prison officials that Oregon Jones got into communications with his brother and arranged a rendezvous with him prior to the brother's break last night." Warden Dalrymple told the media that if Oregon Jones and Milam joined forces, they expected a robbery to occur that was of greater proportion than anything ever before seen in Oregon.

Law enforcement throughout the West was on the lookout for Oregon Jones and Milam. They feared what would happen if they were not apprehended. Citizen volunteers joined law enforcement to assist with the search. Days turned into weeks, but there was no sign of either escapee. The public wondered how two men could simply vanish with so many people looking for them.

It took a year, but Oregon Jones was arrested in Sacramento, California. He had been picked up for petty larceny and his fingerprints gave away his true identity. Deputy Warden Lillie headed to California to bring Oregon Jones back to his namesake state. Once back behind bars, Oregon Jones began plotting his next escape.

One year later, it was time. On the evening of August 12, 1925, the inmates were headed for the dining hall to eat dinner. Four inmates did not enter the dining hall, but instead headed for the fourth tier of cells, closest to the roof. Inmates Tom Murray, Ellsworth Kelly, James Willos, and Oregon Jones put their long-awaited plan into action. Making quick use of their stolen tools, they managed to saw through six boards and part of the tin cover of the roof. They made their way onto the roof, lowered themselves with the ropes they had stolen, and arrived on the front yard.

The four escapees split up into pairs. Oregon Jones came in contact with guard Charles McKinley. He punched him in the jaw and Charles dropped to the ground but was able to get up and grab his rifle.

Meanwhile, escapee Tom thrust his knife at guard John Davison and said, "Give me the keys to the arsenal, or I'll cut your heart out." Davison managed to kick Tom hard enough to push him into a banister and while Tom was getting up, he ran to a guard post and grabbed a rifle. Prison guards who worked inside the prison were unarmed as per policy. Only the outside guards were armed. Tom came across guards Pete White and James Nesmith. Oregon Jones punched Nesmith in the jaw, which brought him to the floor long enough for the escapees to steal his keys to the arsenal.

Now armed with four Winchester rifles, a shotgun, and two boxes of ammunition, the escapees began firing at the guard posts. Guards J. M. Holman, age fifty-five, and John Sweeney, age fifty, died instantly from gunshots. Guard W. E. Gardner went to help J. M., but a bullet knocked the gun out of his hands. Guard John Davison—nicknamed, "Shooting Davison" and "Slaughter House John" for his role in shooting inmates at other prisons—began running towards the guard post. The escapees shot guard Lute Savage as he rushed to a guard post. Just as the escapees were making their way over the prison wall, John opened fire, killing Oregon Jones. His weapon jammed before he could fire off any more shots. Warden Dalrymple, who had been waiting for them to climb the wall, wounded Tom, who still managed to escape.

The three escapees ran towards the state hospital, a quarter of a mile away. Once inside, they ordered Alice Ogburn and attendant McElroy to guide them to the highway. They used the pair as shields as they left the hospital grounds. They saw attendant C. V. Ivitts getting into a taxicab. The fugitives ordered C. V. to get in the taxicab. They climbed in after him and ordered the driver, Zina Zinn, to drive. The escapees continually threatened both men and told them they had just killed two guards. Tom gave directions and they ended up about nine miles outside of Salem before Zina convinced them he was out of gas. Tom ordered Zina to stop the car behind a schoolhouse in the distance. He then told Zina and C. V. to get out of the car. The escapees stole clothing off of both men, tied them to a tree, and gagged them. They stole the few dollars Zina had in his wallet. C. V. had $450 (which they took), before giving him $40 back. Before heading off on foot, the fugitives threatened the men with death if they called the police.

The men managed to work themselves free from the tree and drove off in Zina's car, which had plenty of gas. They found the police nearby and told them what happened. Zina would later tell reporters, "I have seen a great deal of gun display in my time, and have had some thrilling experiences, but never anything like I went through tonight."

Warden Dalrymple reported seeing an ex-convict driving an automobile past the prison gate about the time of the escape. Later that night, a Standard Oil gas station was burglarized, leading the authorities to believe that the trio was close by. The lock on the door had been shot off and a small amount of money was missing.

A posse was rounded up and began the search. The Oregon National Guard, local police, sheriff deputies, forest rangers, and local volunteers joined in the hunt. An estimated 200 armed men, separated into groups, were determined to find the escapees who had killed two prison guards and wounded a third.

Prison guard J. M. left behind a wife, two daughters, and a son. His brother-in-law was Warden Dalrymple. John left behind a wife, a son, and a daughter. Prison guard Lute Savage was hospitalized with a bullet between his fifth and sixth ribs. He was not expected to live, but as it turned out, the bullet did not hit any vital organs and he recovered.

The Oregonian reported:

> Portland today was the unwilling center of the greatest manhunt it has ever known. Hastily recruited police, some of them on vacation, many of them in their beds, were ordered out to scour the town for Tom Murray, Ellsworth Kelly, and James Willos, desperados who casually alighted from an automobile somewhere in the downtown section at 10:30 last night. Railroad officials have called out their special police, and each yard is heavily guarded to prevent escape by that route. A dozen detectives are searching rooming houses in the hope of uncovering the hiding place of the trio. There will be little rest for the entire police bureau until the trio is captured, Chief Jenkins declared. All reliefs will be ordered out and will work double shifts, he said.[3]

Lieutenant Fred Graves told *The Oregonian*:

> There's considerable method in their apparent madness. They show their keenness by capitalizing the dread in which they are held, and it is that very dread of the three men which will make our hunt difficult.[4]

Three days after the escape, Otto Lucht, Joe Lichte, Leo Wilde, and Lawrence Jacobs were at a poolhall in Monitor when Tom burst through the door. Leo later told Deputy Warden Lilley exactly what happened:

The four of us were sitting in the poolroom playing cards. A fifth had just left. We heard somebody come in. Then someone came around the partition, covered us with a pistol and introduced himself by saying, 'Now just sit still boys, keep your hands in the air and you won't get hurt.' The other two then came in and they searched us, finding no guns. They then gathered up some canned goods, took several dollars out of the till, leaving several dollars, says they 'just wanted some change.' Then they took us outside, got us all into Lawrence Jacobs' Mitchell automobile and we started off down the Pacific Highway." Leo told the deputy warden that they ran out of gas on the outskirts of Canby. They ordered one of the men to walk to a garage and bring back some gas. He went on to explain, "When the gasoline was poured into the tank the auto wouldn't start. They became angry and accused us boys of doing something to the car. Finally, it got to working however, and drove on down the Pacific Highway toward New Era. About five o'clock Monday morning we pulled up to C.L. Newman's ranch, which lies a little off the highway on a side road. The occupants of the house were asleep and our kidnapers awoke them, pushed their way into the house and searched members of the family for guns, but found none. They told the Newmans they would not be harmed as long as they did what they were told. Murray apparently was the leader. He was giving most of the instructions yesterday. The convict trio spent the day shaving and cleaning up, rustling food and getting clothes. Except for a few scratches and burns on the hands from sliding down the ropes at the penitentiary, none of them had any particular wounds. Murray certainly was not seriously hurt. About 7:30 p.m. they began getting ready to leave the ranch. They decided to take Leslie Nelson, 17-year-old son of the owner of the ranch, and myself. Young Newman did the driving and we proceeded to Portland. Murray told Newman not to speed at any time so as to attract attention. Before we left the ranch Murray told the others, 'These boys will be allowed to live if you remain quiet and send in no alarm. We will leave them unharmed if you do this. On the way to Portland, we encountered four traffic officers. Each time we passed an officer there was a little tension but nothing happened. After we entered the city limits, we passed several uniformed officers on the streets before arriving at Tenth and Washington. When they left us, Murray said, "to go on and remember as little as possible and you'll come out all right. When you get back to Monitor, hang a curtain on the back window of that pool hall, Willos told us, then we won't be able to watch you as we did this time.[5]

Two days after the escape, Charles L. Newman notified the authorities that the trio had spent an entire day in his house. He said the family was awoken to the sound of their car being pushed out of their garage. Then a car pulled into their garage, concealing it from the road. Immediately, their door opened and the three men entered their home demanding food. He said the escapees had held him hostage in his home near New Era. Charles said the trio had commandeered Lawrence Jacob's automobile earlier in the day. Charles said he questioned them about the prison break. They wrote out a statement, signed their names, and placed their fingerprint in ink on the document. The statement read:

It was our intention to pull the break, just a stickup, we meant to get the guns away from the turnkey, walk ahead and open the gate, or else go through the tower. As it was, five guards were waiting at the gate. They were off regular shift and on special duty. I and Jones were the first to slide down the rope, and we went to the turnkey's office. I had a knife only. Jones had nothing. As I went into the turnkey's office, Dairymple and two guards came out. I let them pass. They were on the run. Dairymple said as he passed, 'It's Tom Murray.' He made no effort to stop me. He seemed to try to get away from me. He knew we were making a break, as I did my best to intimidate them. The guards were unarmed also. He [Dairymple] ran through the front gate and over to his house. Where he went after that we do not know. Right in the turnkey's office there was Slaughterhouse Davison and the turnkey. I knocked Slaughterhouse down with my fist and left him lying on the floor, begging for mercy. He was squealing like a pig, and I backed the turnkey over to the gun case with an open, long-bladed paring knife. Then Jones came in. Jones did not bother Slaughterhouse and Slaughterhouse did not kick Jones. Jones seemed to lose his head for a minute, and instead of letting the turnkey go ahead and open the case, knocked him down with a blow of the fist. Jones was unarmed as yet, and the gun case was locked. Jones ran over to a desk in the corner of the turnkey's office and looked for a six-shooter in the drawer. In the meantime, the guard in tower number one began shooting blind into the turnkey's office. The turnkey ran out at this time, holding his jaw. I grabbed a heavy spittoon and crashed the lock on the gun case, handed a 30-30 rifle, fully loaded to Jones. Jones was excited and began emptying the gun at tower number one through the window. When he emptied the first gun, he picked up another one and did the same thing, but did not register a hit. Jones was running wild. He expected to be killed, and was apparently making his last stand. He was shooting wild. Nobody was hurt up to this time. Jones and tower one were the only ones that fired, except one shot I fired at tower one, but I saw no one to shoot at, just fired at random. I took two six-shooters, a 38-special Colt, and a 32-20 Smith and Wesson. Jones took his sawed-off shotgun, loaded with buckshot, and ran back out on the lawn. When we got out on the lawn Kelly and Willos were standing with their hands in the air under cover of five guards armed with guns, just outside the iron fence, and also covered by the guard in the bullpen, tower number seven. No shots were fired from tower number seven. The only thing which kept the guards from shooting them was that guard Pete White was standing between Willos and Kelly. His being there was the only thing which kept Willos and Kelly from being shot down in cold blood, as a deputy warden told White to get away from them and also told the guards to shoot them.[6]

At that point in the dictation, Charles asked why Pete White was between them? Tom explained:

Because Peter White did not want to see a man shot down in cold blood. He [Pete] came over voluntarily. He was unarmed. When Jones and I ran out of the turnkey's office, the guards that had Kelly and Willos covered ran for cover. Willos and Kelly were still unarmed, with their hands in the air.[7]

Charles then asked the men if they were shooting when they left the turnkey's office. Tom said:

No, I was not, but I would not swear about Jones, but he did not hit anybody. I threw Willos a .38 Colt. The guards had run for cover, scattered towards the trees and the garage. The warden, deputy warden or turnkey did not know where they were. There wasn't any shooting going on right here, owing to the fact that the guards were seeking cover, and we all ran; Kelly, Willos, and I, across the lawn to tower number one. Number One tower was not shooting, and I got behind an oak tree, and I told him to come out and throw his gun down or we would smoke him out of there. Instead of doing so, he kept himself covered as well as he could behind the walls of his tower and tried to get a shot at us with his rifle. As it was his life or ours, I shot him in the head with a .32-20. He fell dead and I made a run for the steps leading up to the tower. Willos was right behind me. Neither Willos nor Kelly had fired a shot up to this time. Just as I went up the first two steps of the tower stairs, Guard Holman, who was concealed behind the iron fence, shot me through the left arm. Just as he shot me, Willos shot him with a pistol.[8]

At this point, the trio began to argue about who shot Guard Holman. Tom continued:

Kelly didn't have any gun until we got inside of tower number one. We had to go through tower number one and drop from that way to gain our liberty. By the time we went through this tower, the bullets were coming fast from the outside of the iron fence and in the garage; five or six shooting at us on the way through. I picked up Guard Sweeney's rifle. We all dropped to the ground outside. Jones, Willos and I were on the ground, and I called to Lute Savage, who was standing in the garage, to come over to where we were, as we wanted him for protection from the bullets from the other guards. He wouldn't come, so I took one shot at him with my pistol. Whether I hit him, or not, I don't know. About this time Jones was shot in the side somewhere.[9]

The men argued about where he was shot. Tom then continued:

About that time Willos and I started for number two tower, along the side wall, as this was the best route for our getaway, Kelly stopped to shake hands with Jones. Jones said, "Tell the boys to play careful and not make it more than one." Jones then took the gun and fired a load of buckshot through Holman's head who was sitting up against the wall. Made him unconscious of what was going on around him.[10]

At this point, Tom emphasized to Charles they were telling "the God's truth." He said he wanted his mother to read it. With that, Tom continued: "Kelly then picked up the shotgun, which was empty, and followed Willos and I [walked] past number two tower toward the insane asylum." Charles interrupted to ask what the guard at tower number two had been doing up to that point? Tom answered:

Number two was deserted, and someone wearing a dark suit was running toward the insane asylum ahead of us. We thought it was the guard from number two post, although we would not swear to it, as we were not sure. We never did notice any shots coming from number two tower, and he could have shot at us when I shot Lute Savage. We rushed toward the insane asylum, commandeered an automobile and from then on, the public knows just as much as we want them to know. We haven't harmed no one and intend to harm no one as long as they don't stand between ourselves and liberty.[11]

The three men signed the document at that point before adding:

P.S. The last we saw of Jones he was sitting on the ground, fully conscious, and unable to walk and if Slaughterhouse Davison shot him, he must have walked up on him and shot him like a dog, giving him no chance.[12]

Charles asked the trio if they could give individual statements. Tom said, "No, this goes for all of us. We all vouch for it."

Charles asked Tom's opinion on Warden Dairymple. To this, Tom replied, "He's as good a man as could be in the position. He's had a hard time during his administration, and he has made the best of a bad job."

Charles then asked John his opinion of the warden. John said, "According to what I have learned from other prisoners who have asked for a chance to make good, he was all right." Charles wanted to know if the warden was a good disciplinarian. John replied, "Yes sir, absolutely."

Kelly was asked the same question. His response was, "I think he is very level-headed, and I think he uses more common sense than some of his subordinates."

Charles asked John, 'What do you think of his actions in the last showdown?"

John simply said, "No other course to follow."

Charles asked, "Was the break executed as planned?" Tom said:

No, we planned to slide down the rope, go into the turnkey's office, put the turnkey and any other civilians who might be in there in front of us, march them straight towards number one tower, using them as a protection, as insurance against being shot at against the wall, disarm the guard in number one tower, taking him with us, if necessary, go to the prison cars, and use that for out getaway.[13]

Charles asked, "You didn't expect any shooting?"

Tom replied, "No, at least we didn't expect any guards waiting for us out in front. We had no intention of killing anyone."

Charles then asked, "Do you figure someone informed on you?"

Tom said in response, "We don't know just what to think, but we believe someone had the wrong tip."

Charles told the police that before the escapees left, Tom showed him a small bottle that he had in his pocket. Tom pointed to the liquid in the bottle and said, "This is poison and I'm going to take it if I'm cornered or knocked over by some bull's gun." He also told Charles that each of them would turn their guns on themselves if found by law enforcement. Tom emphasized, "I'm not going to be taken alive." The three men ordered Charles' son, Leslie, and Leo to drive them to Portland. Once in Portland, they left on foot with their guns concealed in a sack.

Warden Dairymple criticized Charles for not giving up the prisoners. Charles defended his actions, stating that any overt action would have meant death for his family and he was not willing to risk that. He told the media:

The warden has not yet interviewed me in any way about the operation of the convicts. He has made no move to investigate the circumstances and yet he presumes to pass judgment on my actions. It is evident that he doesn't check up matters very carefully. I made an agreement with the convicts when they left my place that if my boy and the young fellow from Monitor who were taken as hostages, were returned to me alive within two and a half hours, I wouldn't turn in an alarm until the end of that time. I had been protecting my family and I didn't want my boy shot because I failed to keep my word. Because I kept our agreement, my family has nothing to fear from those desperate men now; if I had violated the agreement everyone of us might be in danger. However, as soon as my boy returned, within five minutes, I drove to New Era and from there to Oregon City as fast as I could to notify the Sheriff. If I had it to do over, I would do no differently.[14]

Charles stated that the story the escapees dictated to him was true as they remembered it.

The Capital Journal reported:

Sheriff W.H. Edick and Chief of Police William hurriedly organized posses at 9:30 today to guard roads between Hood River and Portland, following receipt of a message from Chief of Police Jenkins of Portland that Tom Murray, escaped convict, was recognized while traveling eastward over the Columbia River Highway with two other men in a Ford coupe. All available men and arms were gathered for a possible battle with Murray, Ellsworth Kelly, and James Willos.[15]

A truck driver reported three men had fired a gun at his truck near Centralia. The truck driver believed the escapees were the ones responsible based on the photographs he had seen in the newspaper. Police did not buy the story though, figuring that the three convicts would not have randomly fired at a moving car. They chalked the incident up to a rock hitting the windshield.

However, once law enforcement learned the men might be in Washington, they sent officers to Bainbridge Island, where Tom's mother resided and they stationed officers along the highway. A police officer thought he spotted the trio near Seattle, so police near Seattle fanned out and a posse was formed.

Meanwhile, back in Salem, the citizens were asking why the prison did not have a siren to alert them anytime a prisoner was on the loose. Employees of the prison were asking why people could come and go from the prison carrying packages that no one knew the contents of. They also wanted to know why there was not a tower at the front of the prison.

A coroner's jury was impaneled, and they began asking questions regarding how the prison operated. One of the jurors asked chapel guard, L. T. Murphy, whether the prison was run as an institution of reform or punishment. He answered the question by stating, "It is more like an old people's home." He told the jury he would probably lose his job over the remark. The jury was concerned why Oregon Jones and Ellsworth were allowed to share a cell, considering they had one escape under their belts already. Prison employees spoke of the rampant gambling that went on, even saying that the convicts could order a deck of cards through the prison office. The employees told how the warden thought the gambling was fine as long as it was confined to "the island."

Reverend C. H. Bryan, who served as the prison chaplain, told the jurors he had informed the governor about the gambling. The governor informed him that he would put a stop to it but he had not even after a second request by the Reverend. Referring to the current administration Reverend Bryan summed up by saying they were "so busy furnishing entertainment for the convicts that it has no time to run a prison." The jury was told that the prisoners had access to hemp leaf and were frequently smoking it. Those interviewed emphasized the lack of discipline in the prison and the absence of morale. It was mentioned that the guards and convicts alike bet on how long a warden or deputy warden would remain on the job. Chapel Guard William Fisher told the panel that, "Discipline is as good as it ever was."

Asa Fisher, yard captain, testified, "Discipline in the yard is good and while there have been occasional trouble the men in general did what they were told to do." Chapel guard Paul S. Frye told the jurors, "The penitentiary is a dangerous place for employees, a menace to the locality in general, and another break is imminent." Prison guard John Davison, who fired the shot that brought Oregon Jones down, told the jury that the discipline in this prison was the "slackest" he had ever seen in his eighteen years working in prisons. In all, five guards testified that the guards had opportunity to shoot the escapees before they headed over the wall, but failed to do so.

The coroner's jury returned with a report stating:

> The four convicts, Tom Murray, Ellsworth Kelly, James Willos, and Bert "Oregon" Jones are held equally responsible for the death of the two guards, John Sweeney and James Milton Holman, who are lauded for their observation of their oaths. Their unfortunate deaths were occasioned by their faithful adherence to their oaths and duty as guards.[16]

Within days of the escape, three guards turned in their equipment and resigned.

Former prison guard Charles Charlton told the media that during the time he worked there, the inmates received three packages of tobacco each week, they operated poker games, they were allowed ice cream on Sundays, there were "plenty of baseball games," and they could listen to the radio late at night. He summed it up:

> Doesn't sound like a place of correction or punishment, does it? I told the warden that instead of being a prison, the place had become a home for the crooks, a paradise rather. It has become so attractive that it is a wonder anyone wanted to leave, and it had no terrors for them. I remember the time when there was discipline, strict discipline, and when a convict was released, he was mighty glad to get away and stay away.[17]

As the manhunt continued, Oregon Jones was laid to rest. A lone floral arrangement sat on top of his casket, sent by an anonymous supporter.

His body was sent to Grants Pass to be buried in the family plot at Granite Hill Cemetery.

While the posses were busy on the hunt, District Attorney John A. Carson announced that he was seeking indictments for murder in the first degree for all three escapees. A grand jury was convened to hear the evidence. It was the first time in the history of Marion County that women served in a death penalty case. The jurors included Mabel Settlemeier, Grace Neiberg, Arthur Girod, George Keech, and L. W. Potter.

After learning of the Monitor and New Era details, prison officials told the media that Tom was one of the cleverest and nerviest convicts ever to escape and they predicted that he would never be taken alive and without a battle unless captured by surprise. That is exactly what happened. Tom was the first to be captured. He had been on the run for a week when he met Phillip Carson in the railroad yards in Vancouver, Washington. They rode the rails to Centralia.

Phillip confided he had just been run out of Portland for vagrancy and told not to return. The two began talking about robbing a store. Phillip took Tom to the Savoy Hotel and bought him a meal. He assured him he had a friend who could get Tom a change of clothing. Phillip left Tom at the hotel and hurried to the police station. He contacted Officer C. D. Pilling. The officer changed out of his uniform into his regular clothes and accompanied Phillip to the hotel. He brought with him some old clothes he found at the police station. Tom changed into the clothes and the three of them began planning to rob a store. Phillip and C. D. told Tom they would flag down a taxicab outside while he got ready. They hurried back to the police station and asked Mayor George Barner to pose as a taxicab driver.

Meanwhile, Chief of Police Compton, Officer Robert Stratton and Deputy Sheriffs Herford and Hawkins surrounded the hotel. C. D. and Phillip went to the hotel room to let Tom know they had a taxicab ready. The three men were approaching the car, when C. D. grabbed Tom who did not resist. He simply said, "The jig's up. I'm Murray." Mayor Barner drove the prisoner to the police station. The authorities wanted to know where his partners were. He denied knowing their whereabouts. Phillip had told the police that Tom had informed him they had all been together the day before in Monitor.

Tom replied, "Willos saved my life when the guard was getting ready to shoot me. I'd be the lowest kind of a rat like the skunk that turned me in if I told on them."

The police tried a different tactic by saying, "If your mother was here, she would want you to turn them in and tell us where they are."

Tom was quick to reply, "Leave my mother out of this, she's a decent woman and has no business with crooks or cops." The police pressed on:

> They may be at your mother's home, Tom. They may think they would be safer there than anywhere else. And if they got there, and the police found out about it, there'd be a fight. You know that. And your mother might get killed. You wouldn't want that to happen, would you? You'd better tell us where they are.[18]

Having his mother brought into the conversation only angered Tom, who snapped, "Now listen to me, didn't Willos kill a guard who was ready to shoot me? Didn't he save my life? I'm not like the bird who stooled on me, and you know it."

He was asked if the letter dictated to Charles was authentic. He said, "That letter told the absolute truth, so help me God. And I wouldn't retract a word of it if I hang, as I probably will." He was asked if he left Portland after the youths dropped him off. Tom simply said, "Listen, I'm a crook, see? And a murderer, and a tough egg. And that young Hoosier who brought me here is a gentleman and an honest man, get me? You take his word for what happened."

Later, Phillip told reporters, "I want to say right here that I never met such a perfect gentleman as Murray. I would not have turned him in but for the fact that he declared I was a menace to society and a lot of stuff like that."

Upon learning of the capture of one of the fugitives, Oregon Governor Pierce told reporters: "Thank God, I am so glad to hear the news, for since I took the governor's chair, nothing has kept me awake nights until the jail break. Murray need not expect executive clemency for he will hang." Tom's mother did not take the news well when an officer stopped by her house to inform her of the capture. She immediately fainted and was reported to be seriously ill days later.

Within hours, Tom was on a train with Mayor Barner, Chief of Police Compton, Officer Pilling, Officer G. E. Reed, Officer M. Rekdahl, Officer Pat Kelly, and Deputy Sheriff Felix Herriford heading back to prison. A small crowd was gathered outside the prison hoping to catch a glimpse of the escapee returning home. As he walked into the prison, he was handcuffed to head chapel guard J. H. Carey and Deputy Sheriff Herriford. Warden Dairymple was waiting for them at the top of the stairs along with a group of reporters. The warden asked Tom if he wanted to talk with the media. He replied, "I haven't anything to say and it wouldn't do any good, but if they want to talk to me, all right." The media did not ask any questions and Tom was led to a cell reserved for those on death row. A heavy screen was placed around the cell to prevent anything from being passed in or out. An armed guard stood at the ready.

In Bingen, Washington, the Skamania County Sheriff's Office was summoned to the Lewis Store for a report of a burglary. Once on scene, deputies discovered the rear window of the store had been broken. The burglars had stolen $18, shoes, a large quantity of cookies, bananas, a pipe and tobacco, and cigarettes. The police located a pair of white cloth gloves that the burglars had left behind. They immediately suspected the thieves were Ellsworth and John.

Further investigation revealed someone had tried to steal the car belonging to the night marshal while it was at the F. V. Flupz Garage. They entered the room above the garage where F. V. was sleeping. They stole his money and the keys to his gas tank.

While the deputies were investigating the burglary, W. S. Rippold reported that his Overland Automobile Co. vehicle had been stolen. Night Marshal Frank Monroe recalled seeing the car leave the highway the night before and head towards White Salmon. Another report came in stating that 10 gallons of gas had been stolen from two nearby gas stations.

The sheriff's office notified the surrounding areas that the men might be heading towards Yakima. Each area began organizing a posse. Sheriff W. S. Warwick reported seeing the car between Goldendale and Lyle. The authorities figured there were three directions the escapees could go. One way was to cross the Central Washington highway through Bickleton and Mapleton, which was wide open country. Another way was to double back and take a ferry across the Columbia River into Oregon and from there take the Columbia River Highway. Yet another escape route was through the hills into the Toppenish country.

When Tom and Phillip were in the railway yard, Tom mentioned that the trio had been together the day before near White Salmon. According to Tom, they had had an argument and he struck out on his own. Armed with that information, law enforcement swarmed the area. Six hours after Tom was placed in handcuffs, Deputy Sheriffs Christopherson, Rexford, and Jackson along with Constable Gloss spotted the tracks of a car that had gone into the brush off Glendale Road. They quietly surrounded the vehicle with guns drawn. Ellsworth and John were sitting in the car they had stolen, eating their lunch oblivious to the fact that they were enjoying their final moments of freedom. The escapees did not resist and were removed from the car but Ellsworth did state, "For God's sake, shoot me quick." He told the deputies he had stolen some poison in a blacksmith shop near Monitor but had lost it the night before while climbing over a fence.

The escapees found themselves in handcuffs, seated in a seven-passenger automobile with Deputy Sheriff Christopherson at the wheel heading back to where they escaped from ten days earlier. Keeping them company on the ride were Deputy Sheriffs Rexford and Jackson along with Constable Gloss. They were surprised at how haggard the two escapees looked. They had barely begun the journey before both were sound asleep. From time to time, they would wake up and chat but then fall back to sleep.

Ellsworth filled Deputy Christopherson in on some of the convicts they both knew. They did fill in some of the details of their ten-day odyssey. They said after Leslie and Leo dropped them off in Portland, they only stayed in the city for two hours. They made their way to the Oregon–Washington Railroad and navigation freight yards. There they caught a rail to Hood River. Once they were in the Hood River, they immediately headed for the forest. The escapees did confirm that an argument had taken place with Tom while they were in Bingen. John clarified:

My determination to break into an old baggage car had nothing to do with the quarrel, for there wasn't any baggage car there. We mixed, not a fight, but just a nasty disagreement, because Tom wanted all of us to get on the next westbound freight. Kelly and I wanted to get east. It made Tom mad and he just simply decided to leave us.[19]

The convicts said they committed the burglary at the Lewis Store out of pure hunger. They did confirm they stole shoes and money from the till in addition to food. Kelly added that he had been sick ever since gorging on all the cookies they stole.

As their journey neared the end and the reality sunk in that they would be behind bars in a short period of time, Ellsworth made one plea:

Tell them that I have never killed anybody, that I have never carried a gun, never shot anybody or blackjacked anybody. I had no desire to kill any of the posses that were hunting us. But I was desperate those first few days and would have gone any length to have prevented capture. I never expected to be taken alive. I didn't intend to be.[20]

Upon arriving back at their prison home, Ellsworth declared, "Thank God, I'll get a good night's sleep tonight." He mentioned he had not had a warm meal since leaving the prison. Officers noticed that John was not as enthused to be back behind bars.

Two months after the escape, a jury found Tom guilty for the murder of prison guard Tom Sweeney. His attorney, King, appealed the decision with an explanation that the state of Oregon could not hang his client until Tom had served his original twenty-year prison term for bank robbery. Before the appeal could wind its way through the court system, Tom committed suicide by hanging himself in his jail cell.

Both Ellsworth and John were found guilty. On April 28, 1928, they were hanged for their role in the murders of prison guard Tom Sweeney and James Milton Holman. Ellsworth was the first to walk up the thirteen steps to the gallows. He was accompanied by Father T. V. Keenan, a Catholic chaplain. The trap was sprung and he was pronounced dead. Ten minutes later, John climbed the same thirteen steps to his death. He played up a nonchalant façade, with a cigarette dangling from his lips. He looked around at the audience, which numbered approximately seventy-five people, and said, "I hope you will all be satisfied."

John had turned to the Christian Science faith in recent years. A member of that religion was with him the night before along with Father Keenan, who stayed with the two men until 1 a.m. Although Ellsworth did not accept the Catholic faith, he found comfort with Father Keenan's companionship leading up to his death. At one time, he asked Father Keenan to pass along a message to John asking for forgiveness if there was any ill will felt towards him. John sent word back that he felt no ill will towards Ellsworth.

Reporters were allowed to speak to the men just before their execution, after they had finished their final breakfast. Ellsworth once again proclaimed his innocence, saying he had never been guilty, "of any of the worst sins." He still proclaimed that he had never murdered anyone. John's final words to the reporters were:

> I am a good citizen and as innocent a man as ever walked onto the scaffold. I did not have a fair trial. As I see it there has been a great misunderstanding. In the future I hope that people will look at these affairs more closely and find out the real cause of men being in this place.[21]

The years went by but there was still no sign of Milam who had broken out of the Jackson County jail. On the ten-year anniversary of Milam's escape, Sheriff Terrill told the media he had given up on the belief that Milam would be captured.

6

America's Most Wanted

In 1949, a reporter for the International News Service asked the director of the F.B.I., J. Edgar Hoover, the names of the "toughest guys" they wanted to capture. The director provided a list, and the names ran in newspapers across the country.

There was such an overwhelming interest in the story that the F.B.I. decided to put out their first ever list of their "Most Wanted" in 1950. They emphasized that no one on the list was wanted any more or any less than the others on the list. Some of the names were on the list for federal crimes, others for state crimes. Those who were wanted for a state crime were on the list because they crossed state lines in order to avoid prosecution. The F.B.I. warned the public that everyone on the list was "desperate and probably armed."

The first Most Wanted list included the name Thomas James Holden, age fifty-four. Thomas was wanted for allegedly killing his wife, Lillian, her brother, and her half-brother in Chicago the year before.

It would take more than a year before a man contacted law enforcement and said he saw a man in Beaverton, Oregon, who he recognized from a picture in *The Oregonian* newspaper. He was sure the man was Thomas James Holden. The witness, who was later described as a "public spirited citizen," led F.B.I. agents to a house in Beaverton. There they met John Roger McCulluogh, who was working as a plasterer at the house. He adamantly denied he was Thomas James Holden until finally, he admitted his true identity once he was at the F.B.I. office in Portland.

Thomas told F.B.I. Agent in Charge Robert L. Murphy that he had withdrawn $2,000 from his savings account and headed west. He refused to talk about the triple murder he was accused of, but he did say he was almost captured twice in the past year, both times while in Montana. The first time was when a police officer stopped him to check the ownership of a radio. The other time was when he was stopped driving a friend's vehicle without a driver's license. He was not arrested either time. He told Special Agent Murphy that he had worked as a carpenter, a dishwasher, a plasterer, and a carpenter/construction worker in Butte, Montana; Billings, Montana; and Phoenix, Arizona.

Within days, Thomas was shackled to Chicago Police Detective Leon Sweltzer and headed back east on a train. Lieutenant John Golden of the Chicago Homicide Unit and Illinois Assistant State Attorney Edmund Grant accompanied them.

This was not Thomas' first run-in with the law. He was known to run with gangster Alvin Karpis. In 1926 Thomas, along with his partner D. Carney, robbed a U.S.P.S. mail truck in Evergreen Park, Illinois. They made off with $135,000. It would be two years before Thomas was arrested and sentenced to Leavenworth Prison. He escaped from there but was captured. Thomas eventually ended up at Alcatraz and was paroled in 1947 after serving a total of seventeen years for the mail robbery.

Thomas was convicted for the murder of his wife's half-brother, John Archer, Jr. He received twenty-five years for the crime despite his plea of self-defense.

7

Omar August Pinson

A posse made up of law enforcement officers from two states descended on Hood River in April 1947. The object of their hunt was Omar August Pinson, who was wanted for the murder of State Police Officer Delmond Rondeau of the Hood River Division. Officer Rondeau was thirty-two years old and had been a police officer for four years.

State Police Officer Rondeau was working out of the Hood River division when something caught his eye. He was either suspicious of a truck parked on the street or he spotted a man attempting to rob a service station. Suddenly, the sound of gunfire pierced the air and Officer Rondeau fell to the ground fatally wounded. The police station was within the same block of the crime so officers arrived quickly. A 1946 Ford convertible sped past the crime scene. The police were able to get a description and a roadblock was set up. The Ford convertible was stopped momentarily when the driver ahead of him was being questioned at the checkpoint. When that car pulled ahead, the driver of the Ford convertible gunned the engine and sped away. Deputy Sheriff Joe Henricks fired two shots, both of which hit the car, but did not stop the driver. A police chase ensued, with the driver crashing the car and fleeing on foot. Police fired many shots but the driver was able to elude the pursuing officers.

At the crime scene, it was determined that Officer Rondeau had fired his revolver five times. Two witnesses heard a total of six shots. The officers working at the crime scene investigated the truck that was still parked on the street. Inside they located two shotguns and three rifles.

They identified the owner of the truck as Omar Pinson, alias John Omar Pinson. Additional investigative work revealed that Omar had served time for burglary in Washington and robbery in Missouri.

Police Chief Howard Hollenbeck requested an arrest warrant for Omar. As it turned out, Omar was only free for a matter of hours before being caught in Ordnance by State Police Sergeant Nevil W. Smith, who fired several shots while ordering Omar to get off the freight train he was on.

The grand jury indicted Omar with deliberate and premeditated murder. Omar waived the twenty-four-hour period before entering a plea and went ahead and entered a plea of not guilty. He previously admitted to Chief Hollenbeck that he was responsible for the death of Officer Rondeau.

During the trial, District Attorney Teunis Myers called twenty-six witnesses. Three of those witnesses were police officers who verified that Omar did sign a confession. During the trial, Officer L. H. D. Sheridan testified that when Omar was first questioned, he stated he had stolen the weapons that were in his truck from a house. Officer Sheridan said Omar told him that Officer Rondeau approached him and questioned him as to why he had so many weapons in his truck. Officer Rondeau asked him to accompany him to the police station to check over the guns. That is when, according to Omar, he fired his weapon. Chief of Police Bill Ross testified that Omar told him that he had burglarized two homes and stolen weapons. He said the homes belonged to Jack Caldwell and Clarence Fitterer. Omar took the witness stand and said he "guessed" he fired the shot that killed Officer Rondeau. Officer Rondeau's parents and his wife, Nerine were present in the courtroom.

The jury returned a verdict of guilty of murder in the first degree with a recommendation for life in prison. District Attorney Wyers tried to convince the court that Omar should be considered a habitual criminal. If he was deemed a habitual criminal, he would not be eligible for parole. He had already been convicted of two residential burglaries in Washington state. Omar's defense attorney, Charles Phipps, fought this, and Judge Wilson ruled that the state attorney should decide.

After serving less than two years, Omar and his fellow inmate, William Benson, were on the move. They managed to obtain a wrench and a saw. They cut through the bars with the saw and then knocked the lock plate off using the wrench. They used a plank from a construction site in the yard and went over the south wall barefoot. A guard spotted the escapees and opened fire but they managed to get away. That night a men's clothing store was broken into. More than $300 of men's clothing was stolen. The next morning, 100 men joined a posse to find the missing prisoners. Some members of the posse went door to door checking all of the houses near the prison.

This was not the first attempt at breaking out of prison for either man. They had each tried escaping before and therefore were being housed in the bullpen, also known as "the hole." Any number of offenses could earn a prisoner time in the bullpen, such as escape, attempted escape, assaulting a guard, drinking prison alcohol, or repeatedly committing a minor offense. Men serving time in the bullpen were not allowed to have cigarettes, mail, radio, reading material, or other privileges. They were not allowed to have regular meals; instead, they received water and a "dog biscuit," meaning flavorless slop. Next to the bullpen were the segregation cells. The men living there did have privileges, but they could not mingle among the other prisoners.

At the time Omar was escaping over the wall, he had already attempted one escape and had been indicted for another. His indictment was for starting a fire on the prison grounds in an attempt to escape. Omar and six other prisoners started a fire in the prison flax plant in the hopes of going unnoticed when the smoke obscured the prison wall. It was not a successful attempt and simply added more prison time for those involved.

Three months after the escape, word came that Omar had been captured in Idaho, only to escape again. The F.B.I. placed Omar on their newly formed Most Wanted list naming him public enemy number four. They cautioned the public that, "Pinson frequenter of cheap rooming houses and houses of prostitution, was arrested August 25, 1949 in Gooding County, Idaho, but escaped in a subsequent gun battle with police."

Tips poured in from one side of the state to the other, but nothing panned out. Back at the prison, maintenance workers were busy installing stronger bars to avoid future problems.

While still on the run, the authorities learned Omar was wanted in Montana after he allegedly did a safe-cracking job in Polson, Montana. Two men who were involved in the safe-cracking job had previously done time at the Walla Walla prison and knew Omar from his time there. The men told the police that Omar was going by the alias of Sam Cignitti. The F.B.I. warned the public that Omar was "extremely dangerous" and usually carried between two and four guns. Authorities believed Omar was traveling with Elmer Payton in Montana.

The men prepare to go out onto Lava Lake.

The bodies of the three men discovered in Lava Lake.

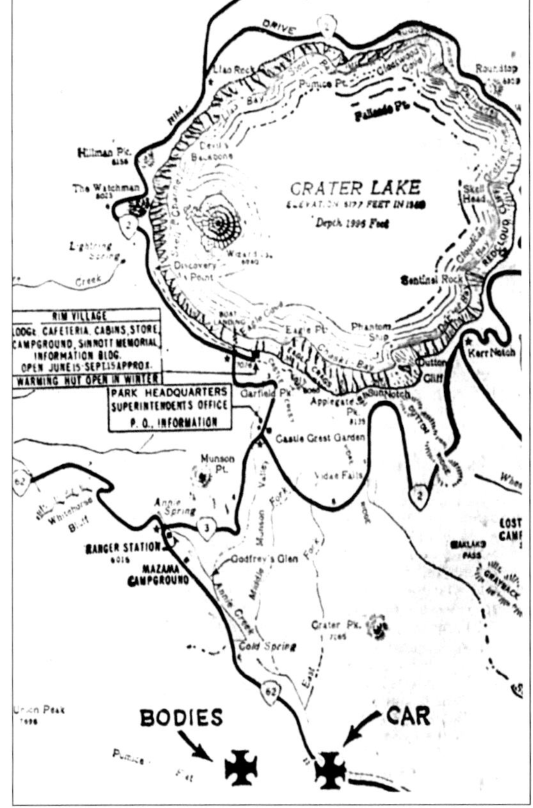

Above: A body is pulled from Lava Lake.

Left: A map outlining where the automobile and the bodies were found.

Oregon State Police
Officer Phil Lowd.

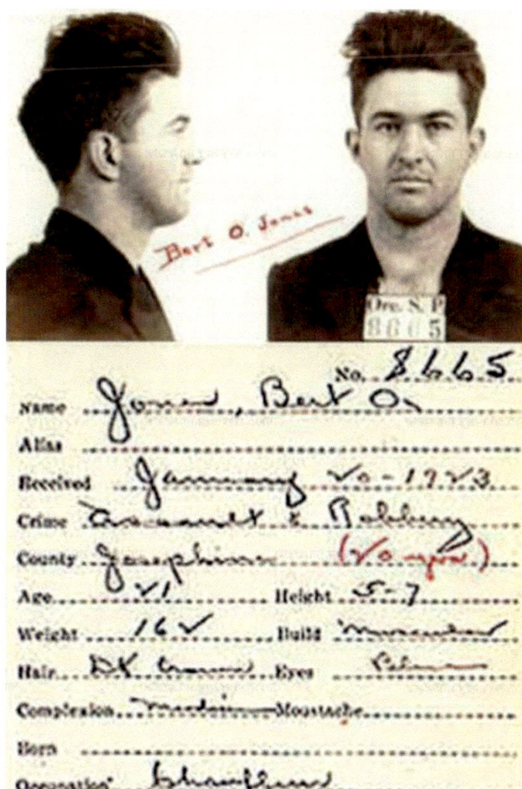

A booking photo of
Bert Oregon Jones.

Left: The Capital Journal shows Tom Murray (upper left), Phillip Carson (upper middle), James Willos (upper right), and Ellsworth Kelley (lower right). In the large picture, Tom Murray is with Officer C. D. Pilling of Centralia and Mayor George Barner of Centralia.

Below: The Oregon State Penitentiary front gate.

One of the guard towers at the Oregon State Penitentiary.

The dining room at the Oregon State Penitentiary.

A vintage postcard of the Oregon State Penitentiary.

A wall and tower at the Oregon State Penitentiary.

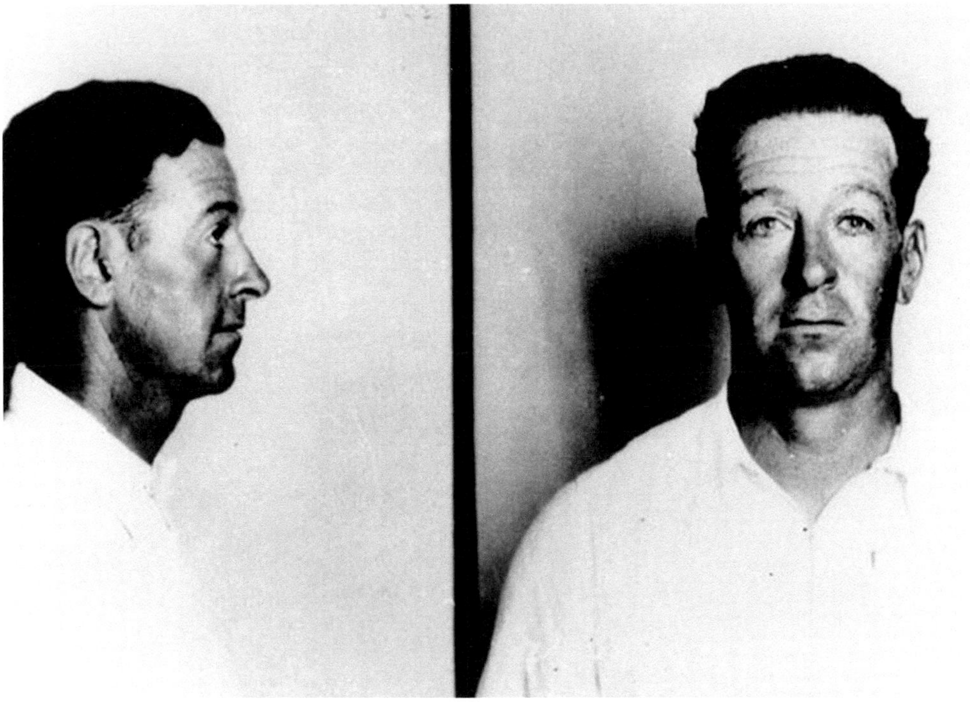

Above: A booking photo of Thomas James Holden.

Right: Omar August Pinson's booking photo.

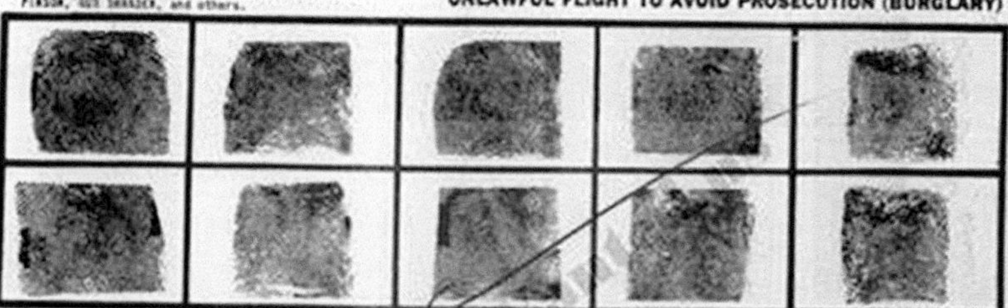

Above: A wanted poster for Omar.

Left: An advertisement for the movie *Gangbusters* based on Omar's life.

Above are two poses of Alton Cov-| mother at Bandon. With the lad| dence which wove the net of guilt ell, 16 years old, who has confessed | is Sheriff Ed Ellingsen, who played | about the head of the boy and his to the brutal slaying of his step- | a leading part in getting the evi- | uncle, Arthur Covell.

Above: A newspaper article showing sixteen-year-old Alton Covell after his arrest.

Right: A wanted poster for Harry Tracy.

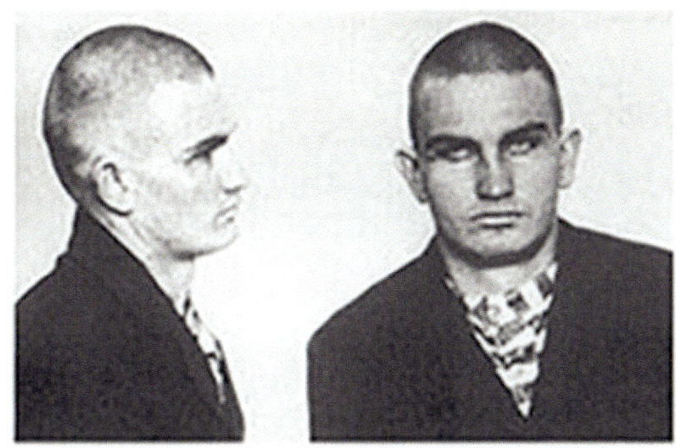

Above left: A photo of victim Dennis Russell with his niece and nephew.

Above right: Edward's murder trial was carried in newspapers across the country.

A booking photo of George R. Kelly, A.K.A. Machine Gun Kelly.

WANTED

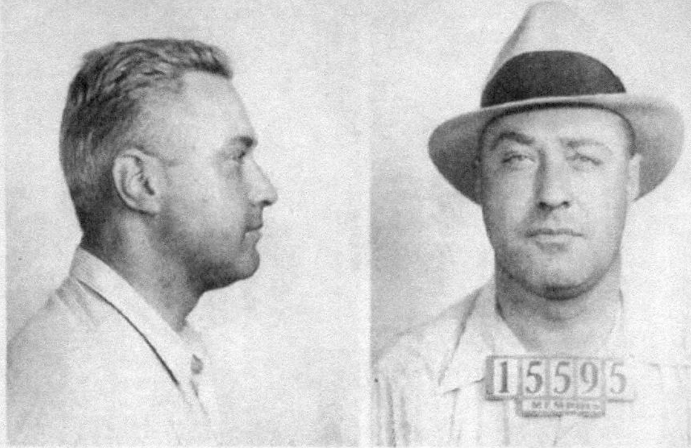

George R. Kelly

aliases

George Kelly, George Kelly Barnes,

"Machine Gun" Kelly

$5,000
REWARD

DESCRIPTION

Born: July 18, 1895 Birthplace: Memphis TN Height: 5' 9-1/2" Build: Medium Weight: 175 pounds Hair: Dark Brown Eyes: Blue Complexion: Ruddy

George R. Kelly is believed to have kidnapped on July 22, 1933, Charles F. Urschel and his associate Walter R. Jarrett. Kelly is proficient in the use of the Thompson submachine gun and should be considered armed and dangerous.

J. EDGAR HOOVER, DIRECTOR
DIVISION OF INVESTIGATION
UNITED STATES DEPARTMENT OF JUSTICE

AUGUST 15, 1933

The wanted poster for "Machine Gun Kelly" for the Charles Urschel kidnapping case.

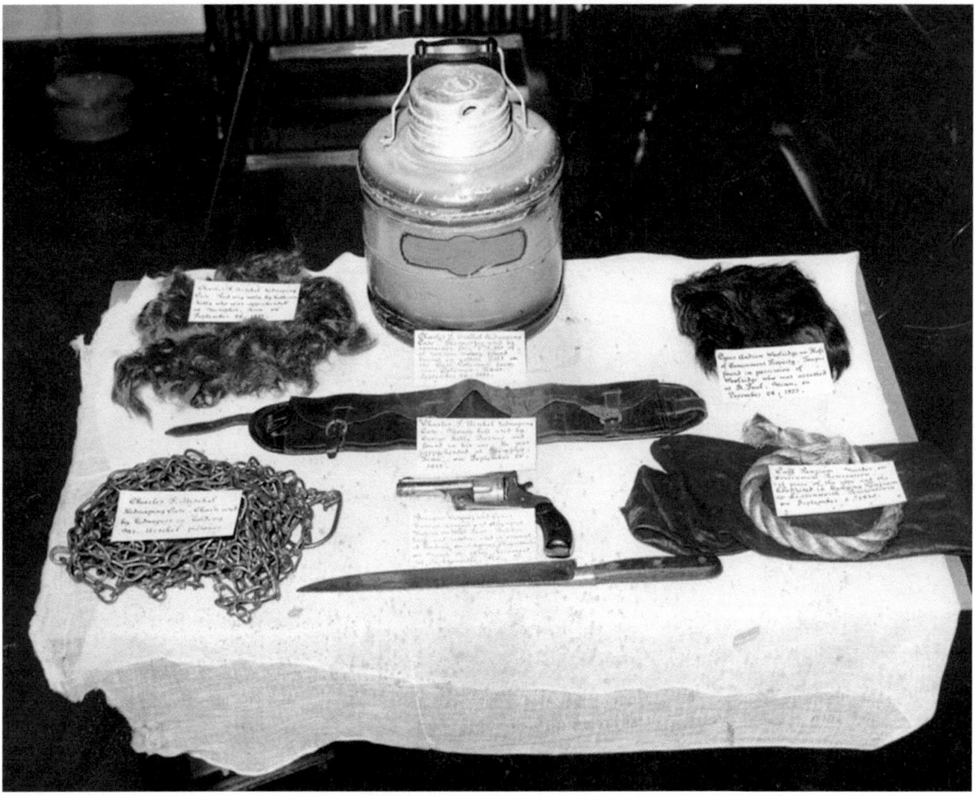

Items recovered by law enforcement that were used in the Charles Urschel kidnapping.

The beige brick home that Charles Urschel and Walter Jarrett were kidnapped from.

Charles and
Berenice Urschel
waiting to testify at
the courthouse.

The Gold Special is shown after the explosion.

REWARD!
$14,400.00

Holdup of Southern Pacific Train No. 13, 1st Section, at Siskiyou, October 11, 1923

FOUR MEN KILLED

...ward of $2500.00 will be paid by the Southern Pacific Railroad Company, of $300.00 by the American Rail-...press Company, and not to exceed $2,000.00 by the United States, for the arrest and conviction of each per-...plicated in the holdup.

...least three persons participated in the crime. Below are photographs and descriptions of three brothers who ...eved to have been connected with the holdup and who should be arrested on sight and held incommunicado.

DESCRIPTIONS

...Roy DeAutremont—Age 23 years: ...t 135 to 140 lbs.; hair medium light ...; height 5 feet 6 inches; complex-...medium light; eyes light brown, ...small; wears nose eye glasses to ...with; eyes appear somewhat granu-...and squinty; face broad, short cut ...long nose and prominent nostrils. ...smooth. No marks. Head round.

No. 2. Ray DeAutremont—Age 23 years; height 5 feet 6 inches; weight 135 to 140 lbs.; complexion, medium light; hair, medium light brown; broad face; prominent nostrils; short cut neck; face smooth; eyes, light brown and small. Eye tooth right side gold crown. Finger Print Classification:

31   1MM   14.
38   0II   17.

Sentenced to one year Monroe, Washington, Reformatory, November 17th, 1919. I. W. W. Organizer. Wears glasses when reading.

No. 3. Hugh DeAutremont—Age 19, looks older. Height 5 feet 7 inches; weight 135 lbs.; complexion fair; eyes blue nose, slightly pug; hair medium light slightly sandy and curly, bleached by the sun; smooth shaven; wore short tan rain coat; also had Mackinaw, but don' know what color.

...e above described men are twin brothers. It is most difficult for those not well ...nted with them to tell them apart. The distinguishing features are that Ray probably ...three or four pounds more and is a trifle taller than Roy. Ray is also slightly stooped ...Ray is more given to talk and pleasantry than Roy, who is inclined to be quiet and ...ming. They have both learned the barber trade and have worked in the woods as ...s and it is probable that instead of being dressed up they may be dressed roughly and ...gers.

...All three men are loggers and may be found in logging camps working as choker setters, hook tenders or whis...nks. They have spoken of taking a long sea voyage and look-out should be kept for them attempting to ship a...orts. They speak Spanish fluently and may attempt to cross the Mexican border. Formerly lived at Lakewood

Left: More than 2,583,000 wanted posters were sent all around the world.

Below: Hugh DeAutremont arriving at the Jackson County jail.

Above: Twins Ray and Roy DeAutremont at the Jackson County jail.

Right: Constable George Prescott in uniform.

The Jackson County courthouse, where more than 10,000 ballots were stolen.

A dedication to
Constable Prescott.

After eleven months on the run, William was captured in Columbus, Ohio. By that time, he was a suspect in holding up the manager of the Granada Theater in Idaho wherein the manager was tied up and the two suspects stole $75. He was also a suspect in a burglary the following night at a hotel in Idaho. He told the police in Columbus, "They might take me back there and I might try to escape again." At the time of his escape, he was serving five years for armed robbery. He had previously done time at Folsom Prison and at the Washington State Prison in Walla Walla. William was brought back to Oregon to finish serving his sentence and for the extra time added for the escape.

When questioned about his partner, William claimed that Omar had died while on the run. William claimed he buried Omar in Salem, saying he had died soon after they escaped. Later, William changed his story, saying Omar had been shot while they were crossing the prison wall and that he "died somewhere in Idaho" from the gunshot wound. He led officers to the supposed gravesite, but there was no body.

As it turned out, Omar was alive and well and living in Pierre, South Dakota. Fifteen months after his barefoot escape, Omar was back in police custody. The mistake he made was going to the Department of Motor Vehicles (D.M.V.) to register a car. The authorities had asked the D.M.V. to be on the lookout for Omar. The D.M.V. notified their state department and Special Agent C. O. Vickmark rushed to their office. He handcuffed Omar and walked him to the local police station. Once there, Omar requested a drink of water. He drank the first cup, then threw a cup in Special Agent Vickmark's face who tried to grab ahold of Omar but he was able to break free.

Suddenly, Omar broke through the screen door and was running down the street with Special Agent Vickmark in pursuit. They crossed empty lots and ran between buildings for two blocks before Omar headed for the front door of a small grocery store. Special Agent Vickmark entered through the back door and yelled at the shop clerks to block the front door. He was able to grab Omar and throw him to the ground. One of the store clerks gave him a wrench, which he held over Omar while waiting for other officers to arrive. When they checked the car Omar had driven to the D.M.V., they found guns, burglary tools, and dynamite. He had $1,309 in his wallet.

Omar arrived back in Oregon handcuffed and chained to Sergeant Smith for the second time in his criminal career. It was Sergeant Smith who captured Omar in Ordnance after his escape. Sergeant Smith and Warden Alexander had taken the train to South Dakota to pick up their prisoner. Warden Alexander told reporters that Omar behaved "beautifully" on the train ride back to Oregon State Penitentiary.

Omar had barely settled back in to prison when he made yet another attempt at freedom. He and William were part of the Halloween escape attempt with Dupree Poe. William was credited for saving the life of a prison guard during the Halloween escape attempt. He pulled inmate Bud Downing off a guard when Bud was armed with a homemade knife.

At one time, Omar did admit, "I guess I'm a failure at escaping." He eventually gave up the dream of the great escape and settled in at his prison home. He began doing clerical work in the records office. He also did office work for the prison psychologist, taught classes to other inmates, and stayed busy making jewelry in the prison workshop.

In 1955, a movie was made based on Omar's life. *Gangbusters* was the first foray into a film after a successful radio show for the producer, Phillips Lord. The part of Omar was played by Myron Healey, and Don Harvey played a police officer on the hunt. The movie portrayed Omar's life beginning at the age of sixteen living in his hometown of Joplin, Montana.

On September 8, 1959, *The Statesman Journal's* headlines read, "Former Prison Kingpin Pinson Granted Parole." The article went on to say that Omar had been a "model prisoner" in recent years and he had been attending pre-release school. Omar had recently said to Deputy Warden L. R. Barnes, "When a man begins getting gray hairs, he sees things differently."

At 8 a.m. on the morning of December 9, 1959, Omar left Oregon State Prison, this time through the front doors. Prison officials found him a job out of state. As he prepared to leave prison, he told the waiting reporters, "I won't be back. I feel very fortunate and very lucky. Right now, I want to forget my past and start a new life." When a reporter asked him if he planned on getting married, he said with a smile, "No, I am not planning to marry. I will have to leave the girls alone for a while." As he took one last look around before walking out the door, Omar turned to Warden Clarence T. Gladden and said, "Thanks for everything, Warden." He again announced that he would not be back. This time, he kept his word. Two years later, the state parole board said he had been a "model of good behavior" since being released.

8

The Covell Murder

"You can say that Mrs. Covell met her death in one of the most brutal murders" is what Coos County Sheriff Ellingsen told reporters on September 6, 1923.

Sheriff Ellingsen and his deputies were investigating the violent death of Ebba Covell, who had lived in a small house located 5 miles south of Bandon. She lived with her husband, Fred, their three children, Fred's disabled brother Arthur, and Fred's two teenage children from a previous relationship. Fred and Ebba's children ranged in age from sixteen months to five years of age. Fred's son, Alton, was sixteen and his daughter, Lucille, was fourteen.

On September 4, 1923, Sheriff Ellingsen, Deputy Malchora, and District Attorney Ben S. Fisher were called to the house to investigate the death of Ebba. They immediately noticed that a struggle had taken place. Ebba had numerous bruises on her body, and it was obvious that the death had been violent, yet her clothes were in pristine condition.

When questioned, Arthur told the authorities that he had been outside sitting in the sun when Alton came and informed him that Ebba had "met with an accident and was lying on the floor." Arthur said he told Alton to bathe her wrists and temples with water and to place her on the bed. He explained that she had been on the kitchen floor.

When the sheriff questioned Fred, he said that he had been at his office in Bandon where he worked as a chiropractor. He said he received a phone call around noon from Arthur, who told him something bad had happened and that he needed to return home. Fred said that upon arriving at the house, he found Ebba on the bed. He worked on her for ninety minutes trying to revive her. When he was unable to get her heart pumping, he came out of the room and told Arthur that she was dead. He sent word to her father, Captain Wiren, at the Umpqua Lighthouse. He then called for help.

The police questioned Fred about his marriage to Ebba. He told them Ebba was his fourth wife; Fred said that the first marriage ended in divorce, the next wife died during childbirth, and the third wife died of cancer.

When the deputies questioned Alton, he described Ebba as being "stiff" when he found her, which led the police to surmise that rigor mortis had set in. That indicated to them that perhaps Ebba had been killed prior to Fred leaving the house to go to work. They found it particularly odd that Ebba's clothing was in pristine condition, yet her death had been very violent and it was obvious that she had put up a fight. The sheriff wondered if her murderer had put a fresh set of clothes on her prior to calling for help.

Based on what he saw at the crime scene, Sheriff Ellingsen took Fred, and his son Alton, into custody. Alton was turned over to the juvenile department. The next day the deputies returned to the house and took Arthur to the county farm to be cared for. The other children were placed with relatives.

When the preliminary hearing was held, Drs. Leep and Gale testified that they had not been able to determine the cause of death. They said that although Ebba had numerous bruises on her body, none of the bruises led them to the cause of her death. The doctors testified that Ebba's neck was not broken, her skull was not fractured, and her lungs, heart, and brain were not compromised. Dr. Leep did say when he first examined Ebba, it appeared that her neck had been broken based on what he believed to be torn ligaments in the first and second vertebrae. After a second examination alongside E. Mingus, they determined that the neck had not been broken.

Dr. Leep testified that Ebba's stomach contents had been analyzed by the state chemist but there were no signs of poisoning. The doctors went on to explain that there were marks on Ebba's face that extended over the bridge of her nose and on the right-hand side from the forehead to the chin. Although they could not be certain, they thought that possibly the marks were made by handprints. One theory was that someone had placed chloroform over her mouth and nose. They described the marks as red in color. Dr. Gale said he thought the skin might have been missing in places on the face.

In order to prosecute a murder charge, the authorities had to be able to prove the cause of death. Based on the testimony of the doctors, Fred's attorney, C. F. McKnight, requested that the case be dismissed. He went on to say that Fred "would assist in any way he could to clear up the mystery." Judge Radley was not swayed and he held Fred on a second-degree murder charge and set bail at $10,000.

Days later, Alton and Arthur signed confessions admitting their part in murdering Ebba. In Alton's confession, he admitted to sneaking up behind Ebba while she was working in the kitchen. He placed a cloth soaked with ammonia over her face. He then carried Ebba to her bed, re-arranged her clothing to hide any signs of a struggle, before placing her on the front porch. In his confession, he described how Arthur called Fred at work and requested that he return home. Alton stressed that it was Arthur who directed him to kill Ebba.

The grand jury visited the county farm to meet with Arthur. After the meeting, they returned to the courthouse and issued indictments for Arthur and Alton. After listening to Lucille's testimony, they chose not to indict her. With the indictments and confessions in hand, the sheriff released Fred from the county jail and dropped the charges against him.

The Covells lived in Coos County at the time of the Ebba's death. Coos County hired criminologist Luke May of Seattle to investigate the case. At the time, Luke was the president of the Revelare International Secret Service of Seattle.

Luke began by interviewing all members of the family. The only member of the family who admitted to being home at the time of Ebba's death was Arthur. He claimed to have been outside sitting in the sun when Ebba died. Although he denied having anything to do with her death, he did emphasize that he never liked her. Arthur had been paralyzed two years prior to Ebba's death after being injured while working on a truck. Prior to moving in with Fred and Ebba, he had been living with his mother on a nearby ranch. At the time of Ebba's death, he was forty-eight years old.

Luke spent a great deal of time trying to decipher the numerous codes and notes about astrology that Arthur kept in his bedroom. He soon realized that Arthur was obsessed with astrology. He even had clients in Hollywood who relied on him for advice about their astrology charts. Luke located a key book that outlined Arthur's future criminal plans. Luke was able to determine that Arthur had planned to kill a total of twenty-six people. The long list of candidates included local people as well as some who lived in Los Angeles. Luke told the authorities that

Arthur planned to kill the subjects when they "came under unfavorable planetary influence." Luke explained to the sheriff that Arthur was an astrologist and a mathematician. In his astrology work, Arthur would use the signs of the planets as a guide that would tell him when to commit the crime.

Luke emphasized that each crime had been planned out in tremendous detail. Arthur had enlisted the help of Alton and Lucille, along with two other teenage children. Arthur's notes indicated that one of the children was to kill Roy B. Carson, who had previously worked at the First National Bank of Bandon. Also, within the notes, there was a plan to kill E. J. Pressey, Pressey's wife, and their three children. Pressey operated a successful dairy. Luke believed that the motive behind the planned homicide was robbery. The notes indicated that Arthur planned to burn the house to eliminate the evidence.

There were also plans to kill two merchants in Bandon with the last name of Sidwell and Squires. Luke was able to examine Arthur's handwriting. He quickly determined that a letter mailed to the local sheriff soon after Ebba's death was written by Arthur. The letter threatened, "You are going to have a rope put around your neck and you are going to be hanged to the nearest tree if you ever speak of the Covell case again." Based on the great details in the notes, Luke told the sheriff that he believed Arthur was of "sound mind."

After decoding Arthur's notes and books, Luke went to interview him at the county farm where he was residing. Arthur did not try to defend or deny his actions. He stated in a matter-of-fact manner that he had indeed made plans to carry out a number of crimes in Bandon. The crimes included theft of homes, stealing automobiles, committing arson in order to destroy any evidence left behind, and to murder a number of men, women, and children. Arthur explained that in some instances, it would be necessary to kill an entire family. Luke later told *The World* newspaper out of Coos Bay that in all his years working in criminal justice, "he had never heard a more horrible confession of crimes planned."

On a cold gray day in November 1923, the trial got underway. Opening statements were made followed by Dr. Leep's testimony. He testified to the bruising on Ebba's body and that both he and Dr. Gale believed that the death was caused by suffocation by the use of a powerful alkaloid.

Next, Fred Covell was called to the witness stand. He told of finding his wife deceased and the grief that he had suffered since that day. When

Lucille took the stand, she admitted that she had known that the murder was going to take place a month ahead of time. When questioned, she stated that she had not made any attempt to prevent the murder because she was afraid of upsetting Arthur. She did say that she did not believe Arthur was actually going to kill Ebba. When asked about the day the murder took place, Lucille testified that she heard Alton go into the house, she heard a struggle and then she helped Alton carry the body from the kitchen to the front room. Lucille admitted there was ammonia in the house.

Later that day, Arthur took the witness stand. He had spent the day lying on a cot in the courtroom waiting to be called to the witness stand. He testified that the only reason he had written out a confession, was to help Alton. He was asked, "Arthur Covell, you heard the testimony of Lucille Covell to the effect that you sent Alton Covell into the house to murder Ebba Covell. Is it the truth?"

Arthur quickly answered, "It is a lie." He explained, "The children came to my room after their father had been arrested. They asked me if I thought their daddy would hang." Arthur went onto to say that Alton said he would take the blame for the murder. Arthur testified that he told Alton that, if necessary, he would take all of the blame, explaining that he "could not bear to see anything happen to my brother or his children." Arthur told the court:

> When I was shown Alton's confession, I refused to make a statement. I read it over carefully and fixed the ideas in my mind. Then I made out my own confession. Ebba Covell's death would not benefit me; in fact, it would have been the reverse. I was dependent on my brother for food and shelter and care.[1]

The Stateman Journal reported that "every eye in the courtroom was riveted on the speaker; every neck was craned for a view of the accused man." Two days after the trail began, Arthur was found guilty of murder in the first degree.

After Arthur's conviction, Fred told the local reporters:

> I am glad that the mystery has been unraveled. It is all horrible to me, but the crime was too heinous to go unpunished and whoever is guilty must suffer. Alton is my own son, but I do not say he should not be punished. I will stay by him to the extent of seeing that he has a fair trial.[2]

Two months later, Alton's trial got underway. District Attorney Fisher told the jury and the packed audience that Arthur and Alton shared a bedroom and night after night, they plotted and planned to murder Ebba. Fisher said that they Arthur chose the date and the hour of the murder based on astrology charts that he had been studying.

Alton's attorney, Grant Corby, began his opening remarks by stating that Alton had been examined by a board of specialists and was found to have the mental capacity of a nine-year-old. He went on say that Alton had never bonded with Ebba and that it was Arthur who had raised him. Grant explained that prior to Arthur's accident, both Alton and Lucille had been living with Arthur and his mother on a secluded ranch. Grant stated that Alton had very little contact with the outside world, other than sporadically attending school. Otherwise, Grant said, his entire universe revolved around Arthur.

Fred took the stand and stated:

> I never could get into Alton's affections. The door was always shut. Alton was bound up in his uncle. Whatever was Arthur's will was Alton's will. Arthur was forever dabbling in mysticism. He was interested in the Hindoos and the mysteries of the past. He was a deep student of astrology, and interested in hypnotism, mesmerism, theosophy and telepathy.[3]

He said that Lucille could be combative and was inclined to lead, whereas Alton needed to be led. Fred talked about a family picnic the day before Ebba's murder. He testified about going to the office the morning of the crime and receiving the phone call from Arthur requesting that he return home. Fred told the jury of the life-saving techniques he had tried on his wife before finally calling the police.

The next witness was fourteen-year-old Lucille. The young blonde girl with a bobbed haircut took the stand. She spoke of eating breakfast together as a family on the day of the crime. She recalled Arthur being in the yard when he told Alton, "It was time." She said Alton went into the house and she could hear scuffling. When he came back outside, he said, "she was pretty strong." Lucille told the jury at that time, Arthur instructed Alton to go back into the house, put Ebba on the bed, look at her eyes, and wash off her face. Lucille admitted to helping Alton carry Ebba to the bedroom. Lucille had previously told the grand jury that she did not know that her uncle and brother had planned to kill Ebba. This time, she admitted that she was aware that Arthur and Alton had been planning Ebba's murder for a month. When questioned why she had not told anyone of their plans, she told the jury:

> I thought it would all pass over. I did not think that they would ever really do it and of course I did not realize what it meant. I never saw but one dead person in my life. I saw a dead man once. Besides my father has a very bad temper and I feared if I told him my uncle and Alton were planning to kill my stepmother, my father would hurt my uncle.[4]

At the end of Lucille's testimony, she said:

> Alton was really sorry for what he had done. After it was over, I was doing the washing and Alton said, "I am sorry I did it. I would not have done it for the world." I said, "Yes, I am sorry you did it too."[5]

It only took the jury forty-five minutes to decide Alton's fate. They returned a verdict of guilty in the first degree and recommended a life sentence.

Fred and the children moved from Bandon. The house sat vacant for a long time. When a fire swept through the town of Bandon, the Covell house was spared.

Two years after the trail, and after all appeals were finished, Arthur was hanged for his part in the murder of Ebba Covell. He never admitted any guilt in the case, but he did say that his astrology chart was off by one hour and that the murder should not have taken place at 11 a.m.

In 1934, Alton was pardoned by Governor Meier with the condition that he reside with an aunt and uncle in Waitsburg, Washington.

9

Outlaws Harry Tracy and David Merrill

Within the walls of the Oregon State Penitentiary, things were fairly monotonous in 1902. There was very little change to the routine, other than a prisoner might be moved to a different cell or a different job. Otherwise, one day was like the other.

The morning of June 9, 1902, was a bit overcast but otherwise, the day promised to be like all the others. A total of 165 prisoners made their way outside to the foundry to begin their workday. Shop guards Frank Ferrell, John Stapleton, and Frank Girard were in charge of the prisoners. Frank led the prisoners into the molding room while John and Frank stayed back by the door. Suddenly, inmates Harry Tracy and David Merrill appeared, carrying Winchester rifles. Before it even registered in anyone's mind what was happening, Harry shot Frank Ferrell in the chest. He exclaimed, "Oh, my God!" He then fell forward and died instantly.

Suddenly, there was commotion throughout the building. Fellow inmate Frank Ingram attempted to grab the rifle from Harry but was shot in the leg, causing him to fall to the ground. Guards John and Frank, armed only with a club, rushed outside to sound the alarm. While they were doing that, both armed inmates fired at the guards stationed at posts one and two. Guard S. R. T. (Thurston) Jones at post one was shot in the stomach. Guard Leidinger was stationed at post two. They fired at him but missed.

At post three, guard B. F. (Berry) Tiffany was briefing guard Duncan Ross before heading to the turnkey's office. The guards were startled to hear a gunshot but before they could react, prisoners were rushing out of the foundry building. Berry ordered them to return but as he did, additional shots were fired towards the wall where he was standing. He was able to get off the wall before another shot rang out. That shot hit Duncan in the right temple. He managed to get off the wall and meet up with Berry. Duncan was not armed, but Berry had a rifle.

By this time Assistant Warden A. C. Dilley and guard Jay McCormick had grabbed rifles and were running towards the sound of gunfire. Up ahead they saw two inmates running while carrying a ladder between them. A. C. and Jay fired at the subjects but were not able to hit them due to the distance. David and Harry put the ladder up against the wall, climbed over, and pulled the ladder up onto the wall to prevent others from escaping. Once David and Harry were on the wall, they began firing at post number two. They jumped off the wall and had just rounded the corner when they came across Berry and Duncan. They ordered Berry to throw down his rifle, which he did. The prisoners used the guards as shields as they headed to a ditch at the end of the prison wall. About that time, guard Oscar Bair at post four shot at the escapees. They, in turn, shot Berry and Duncan. David and Harry ran towards the embankment and disappeared into the thick brush.

The first guards on scene arrived to complete chaos. Inmates were running loose, there were no guards in sight, no one knew if the shooters were still on scene, and no one knew how many people had been shot or how many shooters there were. Their first order of business was to get the prisoners back in their cells. Prison officials notified local law enforcement. Sheriff F. W. Durbin, Sheriff-elect B. B. Colbath and City Marshall D. W. Gibson began organizing posses to join the prison officials who were already on the hunt for the escapees. Within hours, fifty men were searching for the escapees.

Medical personnel arrived on scene and found Frank dead from a gunshot wound through his heart. He had died instantly. On the floor of the guard station, they located Thurston. He had been shot in the stomach. He lived for a few minutes but then succumbed to his injuries. Berry had also died after being shot in the temple. Duncan told the doctor that Berry's final words were a request to see his wife. Inmate Frank Ingram was taken to the hospital for his leg injury.

Frank Ferrell was born in Salem in 1867. He was days away from his thirty-fifth birthday at the time of his death. He had worked for the prison for the past four years. Prior to that, he was a police officer for one year and he had worked in a flour mill as a flour packer. He left behind his wife, his mother, four brothers, and one sister.

Thurston was born in Hubbard and lived there up until three years before his death. His parents were pioneers and settled in Hubbard. Thurston died one day shy of his fiftieth birthday. He was married with eight children. He moved his family to a farm 1 mile from the prison when he started his job as a prison guard.

Berry was thirty-four years old and married. He was originally from Klamath County. He had been a prison guard on the fence for the past several years.

The Statesman Journal wrote:

All of the men were most trusted employees of the prison, and were thoroughly experienced in the work to which they had been assigned, and their loss is felt keenly by the authorities. As citizens they stood high, and the people of Salem and Marion County feel the loss keenly, and the men searching for the murderers yesterday did not do so for the reward, but to bring to justice the ruthless slayers of three of the county's best citizens.[1]

The question on everyone's mind was how had this happened? After some investigation, prison officials believed that someone had smuggled two Winchester rifles and two six-shooters into the foundry room. They figured someone snuck over the prison wall and got into the foundry room during the night. There were broken windows in the nickel work room and the tin shop. It appeared someone had used an ax or a similar tool. They later discovered that an inmate, John Williams, had an ax in his possession but he was not willing to say how he obtained it.

The public demanded answers and were vocal in their anger that two men could obtain weapons, kill three guards and escape. Superintendent Lee addressed the public:

The outbreak was entirely unexpected, and under the circumstances could not be prevented. The two men were supplied with rifles from the outside, probably brought over the wall during the night, and secreted in the place where the tools were kept in the foundry, and where the prisoners secured them. This would be possible during the night, as there is but one guard inside the yard at night. I was not in the prison when the outbreak occurred, but came soon after, and have directed the pursuit. I have sent for a brace of bloodhounds from Walla Walla, and they will arrive at 11 tomorrow, when the trail will be followed and the murderers run to earth. It is an awful affair and I will never rest until I run the fiends down.[2]

Deputy Warden Dilley attempted to explain to the public what occurred:

At seven o'clock this morning we sent the men into the shops, Warden Janes and myself counted them before they went in. Mr. Jayne and I stopped in the yard, after the men had gone into the shop, and discussed business affairs of the prison when the first shot was heard—when Farrell was killed. This was followed by several more shots and the alarm was given. Guards Jones, McCormick and myself hastened to the arsenal, secured rifles and went on the wall, expecting a general outbreak. When we reached the wall at first post, McCormick fired five shots at one of the men climbing the wall. I hastened to post number two where I found Thurston Jones dying. By this time the men had rounded the fence and firing was heard from there. Before we could get to them, they had disappeared into the brush.[3]

Guard Stapleton told the press what he encountered in the foundry shop that morning:

The prisoners had just come in and were going to work at seven o'clock. I and shop guard Girard were standing together about 30 feet from where Guard Ferrell was. The first I knew there was trouble was when I heard report of a gun, and turning, saw Ferrell fall forward with the cry, "Oh, my God!" We saw he was killed and Girard and I ran for safety, through the nickel room for the main building to give the alarm. The convicts followed firing several shots, none taking effect. The firing began in the moulding room. There is no doubt that intention was to kill all three shop guards. There were 165 prisoners in the shop this morning when the break occurred.[4]

As the posse combed the surrounding area, tips poured in from the public. One citizen was sure they had crossed his property. He reported that one man was limping quite badly and the other man was helping him. If they had been there, they were no longer anywhere nearby when the posse arrived.

In Salem, it was reported the men had stolen clothing and a horse from two different properties. They had left behind their prison garb. J. W. Roberts reported to the Salem Police that the escapees had been at his house the night before. Felix LaBranch also reported they had been at his house and stolen some horses.

The next sighting was in Gervais, where they entered the home of August King, who was not aware of the prison break. He told the authorities:

> I was up at 3:30 getting breakfast in my cabin, when a man pushed open the door and stuck his rifle in. He asked me for something to eat. I told him to wait outside and I would get it ready. In fifteen minutes, I called them in.[5]

He described to the police that one of the men appeared to be exhausted and ate very little. Officials believe they were heading to Portland.

The bloodhounds, "Don" and "Hunter," arrived from the Walla Walla Penitentiary with their handler, prison guard N. E. Carson. Both dogs were eighteen months old and had been successful in their endeavors. They were met at the train station by Sheriff Durbin and taken to the place where the escapees had discarded their prison attire. The dogs did pick up the trail, and they successfully followed the trail for a period of time before losing the scent. Next the bloodhounds were taken to Gervais. There they did pick up the scent but lost it soon after.

A posse consisting of 200 men moved towards the heavily forested area outside of Gervais. Two companies of militia were called upon to assist. While they were guarding that area, word was received that the men had been to a home in Monitor. Barney Aker's wife and children were held at gunpoint by the escapees who demanded food. They got away before anyone knew they were there. The bloodhounds briefly picked up the scent at the Aker's home.

Other members of a posse went to Clackamas County to determine if the men had been to David's sister's house. They searched the house and property and reported the men were not there. David and Harry were related by marriage. Harry's wife was David's sister. Both men had lengthy criminal records.

Prison Superintendent J. D. Lee offered a $1,000 reward for their capture, dead or alive. The following day, he increased the reward to $1,500, or $750 per man. He also offered a $500 reward for information leading to the arrest of the person(s) responsible for staging the guns in the foundry room.

The wanted poster read:

$1500 reward for the capture, dead or alive, of Harry Tracy and David Merrill, or $750 for each one who escaped from the Oregon State Penitentiary on the morning of June 9, 1902. Following is a description of each: Harry Tracy: age 27 years, height 5 feet, 8 1/2 inches, weight 160 pounds, complexion medium, hair light brown, eyes blue. Medium built, pit scar above the outside corner of the left eye, pit scar back left ear edge of hair, pit scar right side bridge of nose, vaccine mark outside left upper arm, cut scar inside second joint left thumb, two cut scars second knuckle left index, cut scar second knuckle left fore finger, small cut scar above right knee, two pit scars below right knee, burn scar four inches long upper leg, small pit scar front left upper leg, small pit scar outside and below left knee, dim brown stain bottom right shoulder blade, brown stain on back near spine, varicose veins, hollow left knee. David Merrill: age 31 years, height 5 feet, 9 ¾ inches, weight 137 pounds, complexion medium, hair brown, eyes blue or gray. Medium built, slightly stoop shoulders, dim pit scar below right temple, dim cut scar above outside corner right eye, dim pit scar right side back base of neck, small brown mole left back side base of neck, cut scar on first knuckle right thumb, two cut scars on second knuckle right index, cut scar third knuckle right index, cut scar between third knuckles right third and fourth finger, two vaccine marks outside left upper arm, two cut scars on first knuckle left second finger, pit scar on right knee cap, small pit scar on left side, burn scar on top left instep, varicose veins, hollow both knees, small pit scar below left hip and one above left hip. Also $500 reward for the capture of the man who furnished the guns for the prisoners. Report to J.D. Lee, Superintendent Oregon State Penitentiary.[6]

Inmate Frank Ingram was credited with saving the life of shop guard Frank Girard. As he tried to wrestle the gun away from David, the bullet went into his leg instead of hitting Frank Girard. The warden asked Governor T. T. Geer to pardon Frank to show appreciation for his heroic act. Frank had been serving a life sentence for murder. In 1891, he was accused of killing his younger brother over a dispute about ownership of their family farm. A farm hand was arrested as an accessory. The farm hand was acquitted. Frank's first trial ended in a hung jury.

The next trial resulted in him being found guilty of murder in the second degree and sentenced to life in prison. He maintained his innocence the entire time. In asking the governor for a pardon, the prison officials said Frank had been a "model prisoner." Three weeks later, Frank was a free man. He was still hospitalized at the time of the pardon. The doctors had not been able to save his leg, so they had to amputate it above the knee. Governor Geer told the press:

> During his ten years of incarceration he has been a model prisoner, and for the further reason that during the recent outbreak in the Penitentiary he risked his life in defense of the unarmed guards by which act of bravery he had the misfortune to lose one of his legs. Ingram's prison record is an excellent one, and he has always been considered a model prisoner. While he is now a free man, Ingram will remain at the prison until he can be safely removed, and in the meantime, he is receiving the best of attention. Melvin W.A. Cusick, the prison physician, says the man is now practically out of danger, and that as he is receiving the best care and nourishment there it will be best to leave him there until his recovery.[7]

The citizens of Still Pond, Maryland, were not surprised to read in their local newspaper that Harry had escaped from a prison. They remembered Harry all too well. They recalled that in the early 1890s, he operated a barbershop in their town. They told the media the locals feared him due to his violent tendencies. They were relieved when he left town after one too many fights and never returned.

The newspapers in Utah were quick to report the escape of Harry because it was all too familiar to them. Harry was serving time in Utah for a burglary he committed in Provo. One day while working in the prison rock quarry, he suddenly pulled a gun out of his jacket. Harry ordered a guard to change out of his uniform and to give him his gun and uniform. Harry escaped along with three other convicts. Once outside the prison, they split up in pairs. Harry and an inmate by the name of Lent headed to Parley's Canyon. They exchanged fire with one citizen but no one was hit. They saw a man and his wife in a horse and buggy. They approached them at gunpoint and left them stranded after stealing their transportation. They drove into the canyon and eventually made it to Brown's Park on the Colorado–Wyoming border. Harry was captured in Colorado but not before he and other gang members murdered Valentine Hoy. At the time, he and Lent were running with the Robbers Roost Gang, of which Butch Cassidy was a leading member. He was locked up in a county jail but managed to escape. He was captured but escaped yet again. He was never seen or heard from in Utah after that.

Both David and Harry were serving time in the Oregon State Penitentiary after committing a number of crimes including burglaries, highway robberies, and thefts. M. A. Tuscon, a retired police justice, gave some history of the two men. He told the media that the Merrill and Tracy families lived in Vancouver, but on opposite sides. He blamed David for Harry's downfall, saying in part:

> I am satisfied that Merrill was the cause of Tracy's downward course. Mrs. Merrill, young Merrill's mother is well connected in Portland, but had little regard for the bringing up of her son. The Tracys, on the contrary, as a family were highly respected and young Tracy was thought by all to be a promising young man.[8]

Retired Police Justice Tuscon said he first became aware of David when he was fifteen years old and was found guilty of stealing poultry and selling the birds to a local store. After David served six days, he began to notice the two boys spending time together. He frequently saw them together doing target practice at the local firing range.

As the search continued, the officials began receiving tips that the men had crossed into Washington state. Mr. McCloud rode his horse into the town of Belmore and told his local deputies the men had been at his neighbor's ranch the night before. They had stolen clothing from him, tied him up, and left him. A posse was organized at Olympia and they headed into the mountains in search of the escapees. Word came that the men had stolen two horses from John Rathburn and were headed towards LaCenter or Lewisville. The posse was just an hour behind them and confident they could catch up. However, they soon lost the trail and feared the fugitives were deep in the forest. Skamania Sheriff Totten and Sheriff Marsh set up on the La Center Bridge and waited.

Later that night, two members of Sheriff Marsh's posse exchanged gunfire with the escapees. Bert Biesecker and Lon Davis along with thirteen other men were stationed along Salmon Creek. Just before midnight, they spotted two men approaching the creek. When they were sure the two men were the subject of their manhunt, they began firing. Six shots were exchanged between the parties but no one was hit. The posse continued on, but it was not long before they were shot at. A total of five shots were fired, with four of the bullets hitting the horse and one grazing Bert's arm.

After a month on the hunt, the tips received only spoke of Harry. No one had seen David. Previous tips had reported that he was in poor health, but the authorities did not want to let their guard down by only searching for one man.

There was a sighting of Harry in Kittitas County, Washington. A miner there reported Harry had been camping near Roslyn. Two farmers near Bickelton, Washington, reported being held hostage by Harry, who demanded food. At the same time, another person reported seeing Harry near Woodburn, Oregon. With that news, prison officials put extra guards on duty, fearing that Harry would try to return to the prison and kill more people. They had heard rumors that was his intention and feared he might make good on the threat.

There were additional sightings in Washington. Posses were rounded up and all escape routes were watched but there was nothing to report. That was until Captain A. J. Clark contacted his local police. Captain Clark told the authorities in detail how he had gone to the company house of the Capitol City Oyster Company in Olympia. He said when he arrived early in the morning, employee Horatio Alling was there along with his co-workers, Will Langridge, Frank Scott, and John Messenger. As Captain Clark entered the house, he was shocked to see Harry.

Harry had barged into the house at 5 a.m. At that time, only Horatio and Will were there. Harry informed the men who he was and proceeded to make breakfast. While Harry was in the kitchen, Frank and John stopped by to see Horatio. Harry ordered all four men to stand with their faces to the wall and their hands in the air. They were still facing the wall when Captain Clark arrived and he too was ordered to stand facing the wall.

Harry informed them he had killed David because he was growing "faint hearted." He told how he had waited behind a tree and fired one shot, which brought David to the ground. He then approached the body and fired two more times. Harry explained that the day before he killed David, they had read a newspaper article about their escape. Harry was incensed that the newspaper gave them equal credit for the escape because he felt he should have been given top billing, as David could never have pulled off such a feat without him.

After he finished eating, Harry demanded to be taken to Captain Clark's boat, the *N. and S.* Clark's boat was a gasoline launcher that was docked in South Bay. Harry ordered Captain Clark to start the engine. Harry asked the captain to go slowly by McNeil Island because he wanted to shoot at the guards. Captain Clark was able to talk him out of that action. They reached the Seattle harbor and sat there for a bit before continuing to Meadow Point where they dropped anchor. Harry ordered

Frank to tie up the other men. They were tied with their hands behind their backs and bound to their feet. Harry promised to send Captain Clark some money for his trouble, saying:

> I'll send you a lot of money to make up for kidnapping you and the launch, Captain Clark for I will have a lot of dough pretty soon, and I won't forget you other fellows. You have acted pretty decent to me. Well, so long.[9]

He insisted that Frank accompany him, but he let the others remain on the boat. The two men walked along the railroad tracks for a while before Harry told Frank, "You can go back now." Frank asked Harry what his plans were. He replied, "First I have to get a six shooter. I need one badly. I must have it. I will first hold up a policeman and get his gun. Then I'll go out to Lake Washington and come down to Seattle by Pike Street." Frank asked him what he would do after that. Harry described how he would rob Claney's Saloon and Gambling House. Harry boasted:

> In Seattle I am among friends. This is the only place I can make my getaway. They can't catch me in Seattle. If they do take me, they will have to shoot me from behind, for no man can kill me from the front.[10]

With that Harry extended his hand and Frank shook hands and said goodbye. He later told a reporter, "I was mortally afraid of him; yet he made a fellow feel at home."

The next day proved to be the deadliest in the hunt for Harry Tracy. He was spotted by a watchman, John Freeman. Harry had the opportunity to shoot John, but instead he kept walking with his hand on his rifle. John promptly notified King County Deputy Sheriff John "Jack" Williams, who quickly rounded up a posse. Snohomish County Deputy Sheriff Charles Raymond and Deputy Sheriff Brewer joined the posse as did two men from the local newspaper, Karl Anderson and Louis Sefrit. Several local citizens also joined the posse.

As the rain poured down, they came across a cabin outside of Bothell. Suddenly, Harry opened fire from behind a fir tree. He fired a total of five shots, instantly killing Deputy Sheriff Raymond and wounding Deputy Sheriff Williams. Shots were exchanged between Harry and both newspaper men before Harry disappeared into the woods. Eventually, he came across a farmer in a wagon. Harry told the farmer, "I am a deputy sheriff and one of the men on Tracy's track. I must go to Seattle at once and need your wagon. You will drive me towards the city as quickly as possible; there is no time for delay." Before the farmer could respond, Harry jumped in the wagon. The farmer began driving towards the city.

Later that evening, a young delivery boy knocked on the door of Mrs. R. H. Van Horn's house in Fremont. She was able to quietly tell him that Harry was in her house. He rushed back downtown and told the police. Sheriff Ed Cudihee, Police Officer E. E. Breece, guard Neil Rawley, and insurance salesman J. I. Knight arrived at the Van Horn home. They had barely gotten into position to watch the house when Harry appeared from the doorway flanked by two other men. Sheriff Cudihee did not fire his weapon for fear of hitting one of the men next to Harry. Officer Breece shouted for Harry to throw down his weapon. He had barely uttered the words, when Harry fired his gun, instantly killing Officer Breece and Mr. Rawley. Harry began running and Sheriff Cudihee shot off two rounds, but missed. Once again, Harry fled the scene.

Washington Governor McBride offered $2,500 in addition to the other rewards that were offered in Oregon. Governor McBride requested the assistance of the Washington State National Guard, who brought in hundreds of men to join the search.

A citizen by the name of John Johnson contacted law enforcement and told them Harry had been at his house in Port Madison. After eating a hearty meal, he ordered an employee of Johnson's to row him across the river. From there, his whereabouts were unknown.

Sheriff Cudihee and his band of posses chartered the tug *Sea Lion* and scoured the nearby towns for Harry. As it turned out, he was just outside of Benton, holed up in a house owned by Charles Gerriels. Deputy Sheriff Cook arrived with members of a posse, but once again, it was too late. Harry was long gone. Deputy Sheriff Cook had brought bloodhounds with him. The dogs managed to follow a long trail, but then they came across cayenne pepper that Harry had put down and they lost his scent.

Additional tips poured in from the public. Some people reported Harry had been to their farm demanding food, clothing, and shoes. Other people reported seeing Harry walking along country roads or in the forest. Each time that law enforcement thought they had a good lead, Harry disappeared before they could catch up to him. Other reports proved incorrect and the subject was not Harry.

William Morris found himself in the wrong place at the wrong time. He and his friend L. D. Seal were mistaken for the escapees. William was shot in the leg by a member of a posse. The bullet shattered his leg, requiring two surgeries. He spent fourteen weeks in the hospital.

Warden Janes was summoned to South Bend, Washington, to identify a man who the authorities had arrested believing he was David. Although he did resemble the wanted man, Warden Janes could tell it was not David. The man was released from jail with a story to tell for years to come. Warden Janes stayed in Washington to assist with the manhunt.

The Morning Astorian reported, "William Nixon, of the disorderly district of Seattle, tried to win a woman's affection in the guise of outlaw Tracy and is nearly dead as the result of his foolhardy act." William threatened the lady's life if she told the authorities where to find him. She did not heed his warning, and instead told the police his whereabouts. When the police went to arrest him, a fight ensued and he was knocked unconscious before they realized that in fact, he was not Harry.

There were still no signs of David, but law enforcement learned that Harry was traveling during the night crossing parts of Washington on horseback. They estimated he was covering 30 miles per night. W. A. Sanders and S. J. McEldowney told the sheriff deputies Harry had stopped by the Sanders' ranch the night prior, demanding food. He said Harry kept his rifle trained on the two men and ordered them to give him two horses.

The state of Washington spent $10,000 in one month pursuing the escapees. They searched Clarke, Cowlitz, Lewis, Thurston, Pierce, Kitsap, Snohomish, and King counties, but had nothing to show for their efforts.

There was some excitement when the authorities learned that Harry was cornered in a shack near Ravensdale, but if he had ever been there, he was long gone. A fire was still smoldering in the fireplace. The bloodhounds were sent in but to no avail.

Six weeks after the escape, Mary Wagner and her twelve-year-old son were walking to her daughter's house when she smelled a stench that took her by alarm. She walked a short distance into a field and spotted a badly decomposed body. She notified the authorities and they believed it was David Merrill. He had been shot a total of three times. Three 30.30 Winchester shells were found near the body. In investigating the crime scene, the deputies believed Tracy ambushed David, shooting him once to fell him and then coming up close and shooting him two more times.

Superintendent Lee stood by to receive the remains of David Merrill at the prison. The casket was opened and the body was identified, which was difficult due to the condition of the remains. The casket was sealed and lowered into the prison cemetery. Accompanying the remains were Mary Wagner, Sheriff Edward Deggeller, and Warden Joseph Janes. Superintendent Lee explained to Mary Wagner that she would not be entitled to the reward money, but he would reimburse her for her expenses. She argued that she was entitled to the $1,500. Superintendent Lee reminded her that the money was for both men and he could not pay her a reward because she had not captured David, merely come across his body after he had been killed. He offered her $300 to cover her expenses. She refused the reimbursement money and instead filed a formal complaint with the governor. In the end, her claim was denied.

News came that Harry had been seen near the Matchez Pass leading over the mountains onto the Yakima Valley. Then word came that Harry was near Creston, Washington. A youth by the name of G. E. Goldfinch, age eighteen, rushed into the town of Creston and relayed a telegram to the sheriff's office, saying that Harry was at the Eddy ranch. When they contacted him, he explained that he was on horseback about 10 miles south of Creston when he noticed a man on horseback trying to get his attention. The man said his name was Harry Tracy and he asked where the nearest ranch was.

G. E. told Harry the Eddy ranch was nearby and offered to take him there. Once at the house, Harry cleaned up and ate dinner with the Eddy family and G. E. The next morning, Harry went out to the barn and helped Eddy and his farmhands build an overhead track in the barn. While still holding his largest pistol, he allowed the others to inspect his other revolver and his rifle. He then enlisted G. E.'s help with making a new holster out of some leather in the barn. Towards the end of the morning, Harry told G. E. that he would allow him to leave the ranch, but threatened him with death if he told the authorities. G. E. wasted no time in notifying the local sheriff.

Deputy Sheriff C. A. Straub, Melvin E. C. Danter, Attorney Maurice Smith, railroad foreman J. J. Morrison, and Frank Lillengren formed their own posse and set off in search of Harry. They split into two groups to surround the Eddy barn, where he had been spotted. There was a slight hill near the barn where they could stand and survey the land. They spotted Harry unhitching horses and could tell that he had his revolvers but not his rifle.

"Who are those men?" asked Harry.

In reply, Eddy simply said, "I don't see any men." Harry looked again towards the hill. At that moment, men came from the barn door yelling, 'Hold up your hands." Harry instantly jumped behind Eddy, shouting at him to get into the barn. Using Eddy as his shield he managed to get closer to the stable where his rifle was. He grabbed his rifle and began running. He fired two shots towards the men but missed both of them. Harry took off running but so did the posse. Harry came to a boulder that he took cover behind. He rested his rifle on the boulder and fired eight rounds towards the posse, but again, he missed. The posse continued firing at their target. Harry began running towards a wheat field but he tripped, falling face first into the wheat. He began crawling on his hands and knees.

The posse saw Harry enter the wheat field, but by this time, daylight was fading fast. They feared if they followed him into the wheat field, it would be an ambush and they might not survive. They decided to surround the wheat field that night and wait for daybreak. Sheriff Gardner arrived on scene along with Spokane Police Officers Stauffer and Gemmrim, Police Officer Jack O'Farrell of Davenport, and citizens from nearby communities. The posse told the new arrivals that they had heard a gunshot soon after Harry went into the wheat field but they had not seen him since he entered the field.

The day of August 9, 1902, dawned under a bright summer sky full of promise for the posse to finally capture their man. When the sun was high enough on the horizon, they made their way into the wheat field, guns at the ready. They had barely entered the field when they came across the body of the man who had terrorized so many, lying dead among the stalks of wheat. He had used his own 45-caliber revolver to shoot himself in the head. He was lying on his side, with one hand was on the revolver; the other hand on the rifle. The body was cold to the touch, leading the men to believe the gunshot they heard the evening before was Harry committing suicide as his capturers closed in.

At closer examination, they saw Harry had suffered two gunshot wounds to his left leg. One shot had broken the leg between the ankle and the knee. The other shot cut through his artery. They could tell he had tried to stop the bleeding by tying a belt around his leg. The men realized that when they were firing at him as he ran, they actually did hit him in the leg. Originally, they thought Harry had tripped and then began crawling in an attempt to stay low. Now they realized he had suffered a gunshot wound to his leg and was only able to crawl. They figured Harry came to the realization that he was never going to be able to get away with his injured leg and decided not to prolong his agony and shot himself in the head, thus ending a manhunt that stretched two months and through two states. Maurice was credited with firing the shot that wounded his leg.

Before the news broke of Harry's death, an impersonator armed with a rifle and two revolvers showed up at the farm house of N. B. Gilliam, near Medical Lake demanding some food. The fraudulent Harry was riding a horse and claimed to be the authentic Harry Tracy. When the homeowner expressed some doubt, he happily replied, "If you don't believe I am Tracy, I'll show you." He proceeded to fire his weapons off in the distance. The impersonator ate some dinner and then a companion showed up saying, "It's time we were going, Harry." With that they rode off together. The impersonator's next stop was outside of Cheney, where he stole a saddle horse from a Mr. Hathaway.

The five members of the posse from Creston shared the reward money. The town of Creston had a story to tell for generations.

Preparations for returning Harry's body to Salem were underway when they began receiving requests that they make stops along the way so the public could view the body. The reply came swiftly:

> We will not stop at any of the stations. We are going under the instructions of Coroner Moore, and he has ordered the coffin sealed. His instructions are that we not to make any stops, only where it is absolutely necessary.[11]

Accompanying the body from Moscow, Washington were Deputy Sheriff Straub, Melvin A.C. Lantner, and Maurice Smith.

Once the body arrived at the prison, it was handed off to Superintendent Lee at the railroad yard. The wooden box was opened so that a positive identification could be made. Superintendent Lee, Warden James, and other prison employees positively identified the body, as did a number of inmates. They placed Harry's remains in the prison chapel so that his fellow inmates could pay their respects. Next, they poured sulfuric acid on the remains to deter the public from digging up the remains and putting them on display. The box was transferred to the prison cemetery and placed in the ground next to other inmates who never made it out of prison.

Charles Monte and Harry Wright were indicted on murder in the first degree after it was determined they were responsible for arranging for guns to be hidden in the foundry room. Numerous witnesses testified that Charles and Harry, who had been released shortly before the prison break, scaled the prison wall the night before and placed the weapons in the foundry room. In Charles' trial, the jury returned a verdict of guilty of murder in the second degree for the death of prison guard Frank Ferrell. Harry's trial resulted in a hung jury after eighteen hours of deliberations. The sticking point was conflicting testimony as to whether he was living in Washington or in Salem at the time of the prison break. Many Oregonians were surprised when Governor West announced he was issuing a pardon for Charles for his role in procuring the guns used in the prison escape. He cited the "circumstantial and flimsy evidence." Charles walked out of prison a free man.

After being released from the prison hospital, Frank Ingram moved to California. Friends of Woodland gave him a start. He died fourteen years after the escape. In his will, he asked the executrix of his estate (valued at $800 plus a lot in Oakland) to retrieve his leg from the prison in Oregon and bury it with his body. He requested the state of Oregon cover the expense. He had severed all ties with his family after he was convicted of murdering his brother. He did leave funds to cover the perpetual care of his mother's grave in Salem.

10

A Headless Corpse

Oregonians opened their newspapers in July 1921 to see the headline: "Mystery Shrouds Automobile Accident. Dr. Brumfield and Dennis Russell missing; decapitated body under auto."

The citizens of Roseburg were gathering in the streets, hoping to find out more details about the accident that occurred just outside of their town. Rumors were spreading that their town's dentist had been murdered and his car driven down an embankment to cover it up. Others believed Dr. Richard "Melvin" Brumfield was responsible for murdering Dennis Russell, who no one could locate. The media was pressuring the local law enforcement for details, but they were just as puzzled as everyone else.

What the sheriff's office did know was that Lloyd Davis and Daney Campbell were on their way home from a picnic the night of July 13, 1921, when they saw flames shooting in the air. The boys could see there was a car on fire down an embankment on Melrose Road. They went into Roseburg and saw James Fletcher and Bill Dolan, who agreed to accompany Daney to the scene. They were able to get close enough to see that there was a body beneath the overturned car. They went back to town and notified Deputy Sheriff Webb, who in turn notified Coroner Ritter. Once the deputy sheriff and the coroner arrived at the scene, they saw a charred, headless body at the bottom of the embankment near the car. Using ropes, they hoisted the headless body to the top of the embankment and then went in search of more bodies. They did not locate any additional bodies, but they did find pieces of scalp from their victim. The body was taken to the morgue for closer examination.

The deputies determined that the Elgin Six Touring Automobile belonged to Dr. Melvin Brumfield, a dentist in Roseburg. They surmised that the car was traveling at a high rate of speed, it left the road, plunged over the embankment, struck the bottom of a gulch, and burst into flames. The body was badly burned. There were three sticks of dynamite near the car, which led the deputies to believe an explosion had taken place, decapitating the body. While searching the area surrounding the car, deputies located keys, several letters, a registration card, and a gold watch. The next day, when they did a more thorough search, they located a black vest that was badly burned, a few coins in the pocket of the vest, finger nail clippers, a cigarette holder, a black pipe, and several more pieces of the victim's scalp. Inside the car, they found a badly burned rifle.

Coroner Ritter and Deputy Sheriff Webb went to the Brumfield home and woke up Mrs. Brumfield to tell her the news of the automobile accident. They asked where her husband was and she told them he had not come home from work when she went to bed at 11 p.m. She told them he had phoned that evening and said he would be working late. When she asked what time he would be home, he told her it would be "Perhaps nine, ten, or eleven o'clock." She said she usually waited up for him when he worked late, but she was too tired to do so and decided to go to bed.

A few people recalled seeing Melvin at the Rose Candy Kitchen about 6 p.m. the night of the accident. The elevator operator at the Perkins building remembered Melvin arrived at around 8:30 p.m. and needed to go to his office on the third floor. He asked the elevator operator to hold the elevator so he could dash into his office. The elevator operator told the police that when Melvin reappeared, he was carrying "several bundles." Other people reported seeing Melvin on Pacific Highway near Dillard between 8 and 9 p.m. on the night in question. The people who say they saw him told the authorities he was driving in an aggressive manner. More than one person noticed Melvin was having difficulty with the headlights on his car. Another person said he saw Melvin driving in Roseburg at 10 p.m. that night. Police Officer Edward Kohlagen reported seeing Melvin speeding down Main Street. He held up his hand signaling for Melvin to stop, but he continued driving at a high rate of speed.

Mrs. Brumfield was brought to the morgue to identify the remains of the badly charred body. She recognized the ring on a finger and confirmed the body was her husband. She said the signet ring was from his fraternity and had great significance to him. Fred Haynes also confirmed that the body in question was Melvin. Melvin's barber, Ray Buell, examined the pieces of hair attached to the remains of the scalp and said that it belonged to Melvin.

However, Deputy Sheriff Webb was not convinced that the body was Melvin. He noted that the scalp held patches of gray hair, but Melvin's hair was black. There were white socks on the body, yet Mrs. Brumfield said her husband only wore black socks. He also found it troubling that there were documents at the crime scene that belonged to Dennis Russell. Dennis' brother looked at the body and said that it was not his brother.

Constable Dillard, Sheriff Sam Starmer, and Deputy Sheriff Webb went to Dennis's cabin. Dennis was known as a hermit who lived alone in a small cabin on the Pacific Highway just outside of Roseburg. Upon entering the cabin, they immediately noticed the bed had not been slept in and there were no signs of Dennis on the property.

Later that day, Sheriff Starmer was asked to respond to an area near Dillard where a large pool of blood had been located along with a hat. The person who found the blood, Grant Clayton, had originally concluded that the scene was from a hunting party who had killed a deer. When word came of the dead body, he decided to notify the authorities. Sheriff Starmer and County Judge Quine arrived at the location and found the pool of blood and the hat. The pool of blood was so large that it led them to believe that a violent crime had taken place. In examining the hat, Sheriff Starmer believed that the victim had been hit over the head with a blunt instrument and then shot with a rifle. The band of the hat had the initials, W. D. R. Dennis went by his middle name but his first initial was "W."

Based on the new evidence, Sheriff Starmer returned to his office and began making flyers that stated Melvin Brumfield was wanted in questioning for the murder of Dennis Russell. A $200 reward was offered. *The News-Review* out of Roseburg reported:

> Excitement was at white heat on the streets of Roseburg tonight and hundreds of people congregated in groups along the business district discussing the murder and the man hunt for Melvin Brumfield. All seem anxious for his apprehension and many have signified their willingness to the officers to assist in the search.[1]

Details began to surface that Melvin was heavily in debt. The deputies learned he had borrowed $500 and then $600 in the days leading up to the car crash. Their research showed he had purchased dynamite days before the accident, saying he needed to blow up some tree stumps on his property. Further investigation showed that Melvin had a $10,000 accident insurance policy, a $16,000 life insurance policy, and a $1,000 automobile insurance policy. The investigators learned the Brumfields had moved to Roseburg from the east coast about twelve years prior to this incident. Their research showed that the Brumfield's city home, valued at $6,000, had been destroyed in a fire within the past few years. They also learned that the Brumfield's country home went up in flames. A friend of Melvin's told Sheriff Starmer that Melvin had a nervous breakdown a few years before this incident.

Five days after the discovery of the body, a jury was impaneled for a coroner's inquest. Practically the entire town of Roseburg arrived at the courthouse. Hundreds were turned away due to the capacity of the courtroom. The local newspaper reported that there had never been so much interest in one criminal case. Mrs. Brumfield arrived wearing a heavy black veil. She was accompanied by her friend, Mrs. C. S. Heinline. She had been staying with the Heinlines since the accident. Sitting on the jury were Robert Kidd, John Throne, O. C. Baker, Napoleon Rice, Barton Helliwell, and Paul Bubar.

As the case got underway, it became apparent that the case was going to be anything but easy. Not only could the prosecutors not say for certain who the body belonged to—Melvin or Dennis—but they also could not prove how the person died. Four theories were presented; being shot, an automobile accident, dynamite, or the resulting fire.

District Attorney George Neuner had been in Los Angeles, California, for an Elks convention when he first learned of the case. While on a train heading to visit friends in Fresno, he picked up a Los Angeles newspaper. He did a double take when he realized his hometown was plastered across the headlines. He took the first train back to Roseburg and began studying the case.

Those who had fought their way into the courtroom were elated to be present when the first witness was called; Mrs. Brumfield. She gave some family background information, saying that her husband was thirty-eight years old and they had three children. She said her husband graduated from a dental college in Chicago and they moved to Roseburg soon after, arriving in 1911. Mrs. Brumfield told the jury:

I last saw my husband on the morning of July 13. I talked with him later in the day by telephone. He called me at noon and again at about six o'clock p.m. He told me he wouldn't be home until late in the evening and would eat a lunch in town. He had not been feeling well since Sunday, he was troubled with his stomach. On Sunday before the accident, we visited the Meredith homestead. My three boys went out into the hills with the men during the day. We returned to our home that evening. I have never noticed anything wrong with my husband lately. He always tried to get home from work as early as possible, from 5:00 to 5:30 p.m.[2]

Mrs. Brumfield testified that she was positive the body that she saw at the morgue was her husband. When asked about her husband's descriptors, she said:

The doctor was six feet in height. He was dark complexioned and weighed 182 pounds. He wore a 15 ½ sized shirt, and a shoe about 8 ½ in size. He wore no special make of shoes. He had no special marks or scars on his body. He had dark hair, some part of it gray. He wore a fraternity ring-the only one he ever possessed.[3]

District Attorney Neuner handed her a ring that she identified as belonging to her husband. She also identified a burned portion of a necktie, a scarf pin, a leather key case, and a knife as all belonging to her husband. She went on to say:

He possessed an Elgin watch. He had a tie pin Fleur de Lis shaped with a diamond chip. He had no Oxford shoes. He has been wearing black shoes this summer. The doctor had a .30 automatic. It was in the car on Sunday on our trip. He had no other firearms. It was carried in a hunting case. We made two trips to the Meredith homestead. On our first trip to the homestead, we met Dennis Russell. He had dinner with us. Melvin had no conversation with Mr. Russell about any work to be done on our place.[4]

She told the jury that the body in the morgue could not be Dennis' because she had met him, and his body type was much different than that of her husband. She emphatically stated, "Of course I am positive that it is the doctor's body." It was her belief that Dennis murdered her husband because he usually carried up to $1,000.

The young boys who were the first to see the flames testified as to what they saw. Coroner Ritter testified as to his findings: "I found the body without a head, lying about three feet from the car. It was badly charred." He showed the jury the pieces of scalp with the hair attached. He also introduced bits of a pair of bib overalls, pieces of a burned gun stock, a pair of burned white socks, two white handkerchiefs; one with the letter "W," a blue coat, a knife, a tire gauge, and a belt buckle with the letter "B." He showed the jury fragments of a bullet he had recovered from the body. The jurors showed great interest when Coroner Ritter introduced the badly burned ear that was attached to a piece of scalp that still had some gray hair on it. He also brought in a branch that had blood and brain material on it. Additionally, two sticks of dynamite that were at the crime scene were introduced.

Melvin's last patient of the day, Glenn Eddings, testified that he had invited the dentist to go swimming but he declined, saying he had to get home. Other patients and citizens of Roseburg testified to knowing the dentist. Some testified to seeing him driving on the night in question. Officer Kohlagen testified about seeing the dentist speeding down Main Street.

Mr. Selig took the stand and testified that the shoes that were on the body were exactly like the ones Dennis had purchased from the general store that he owned in Myrtle Creek. District Attorney Neuner showed Mr. Selig the shoes taken from the body, and he confirmed they appeared to be the ones he had sold to Dennis. Among the documents found near the car was a card showing the purchase of a pair of shoes by Dennis at the Selig Store in Myrtle Creek.

All eyes were on Grant Clayton when he took the stand and told of finding a pool of blood measuring approximately 5 feet long and 2 feet wide along the road by Dillard. He said when he went back to examine the blood after deciding it was not from a deer, he found bits of a scalp bone with hair, a small piece of a cooper jacket, and a fragment of a bullet. He said he was an acquaintance of Dennis' and had seen him the morning of the incident wearing bib overalls. Grant told the jurors, "I saw the body at the morgue on Friday and it was Dennis."

Mrs. Burchard testified that Melvin came into her store, Burchard Dry Goods, in the late morning of July 13, 1921. She said he had been in the store the previous day and was looking at a pink skirt. Now, on July 13, there was a lady in the store, looking at that same skirt when Melvin came in requesting an empty box; Mrs. Burchard directed him to the back of the store. Melvin nodded to the lady looking at the pink skirt. In the back of the store, Melvin picked up a box containing woman's lingerie and several books, one of which had the name, Norman Whitney, who was a relative of Mrs. Burchard's. She testified that he took the box and exited by way of the back door, without saying another word.

An employee of Southern Pacific Railroad, J. H. Hogan, testified that the day prior to the incident, Melvin was at the Myrtle Creek Express Office. He wanted to send a package to Banff, Canada. The package was addressed from Brumfield to Norman Whitney. The express agent, H. H. Tibbills, was not able to tell him the price to Canada, so Melvin asked that the package be sent to Seattle, where his wife would pick it up.

Kenneth Ronk testified to having known Dennis for a long period of time. He recalled hearing a gun shot from the direction of Dennis' cabin and then seeing a car pass by. He described the car as sounding, "like an airplane." He said after learning of the accident, he went to the location where he thought the gun shot came from and he saw a piece of scalp. He later gave the piece of scalp to Millard Meredith.

Millard Meredith took the stand and explained that he was a nephew of Melvin's. He was familiar with both Melvin and Dennis. He gave descriptions of each to the jury. He stated the first time he saw the body in the morgue, he believed it was not Melvin, but later he changed his mind and said it was. He said Kenneth did give him a part of the scalp, but he gave it to Sheriff Starmer.

After hearing testimony from multiple witnesses, the coroner's jury returned a verdict that the body was that of W. Dennis Russell. They believed he had been killed by a gunshot to the head while along the Pacific Highway. The verdict did not sway those who still believed the body belonged to Melvin Brumfield.

The one thing that did sway the holdouts was when Melvin Brumfield was captured a month later in Canada. The long arm of the law found him working on a ranch in Calgary, Alberta. The Canadian Northwest Mounted Police and the Calgary City Police arrived on the property and took him into custody without incident. Melvin had been living under an assumed name—Norman Whitney. At first, he tried to deny his true identity but then admitted he was Melvin Brumfield. News of his arrest made national news.

Everyone who had followed the mystery wanted to know how the police had located the missing dentist. Sheriff Starmer explained that when Melvin went to the Southern Pacific Railroad Express Office in Myrtle Creek, he asked to have his package shipped to Canada. Although, they could not accommodate his request, they did send the package to Seattle. Later, the employees at the Seattle office received a letter from Mrs. Norman Whitney from Banff, asking that the package be sent to

Banff. By this time, the employees had read newspaper articles about the strange case and decided to contact the authorities. The police collected the package and then contacted the authorities in Banff to ask that they determine if a man by the name of Norman Whitney had recently arrived in their area. When the police in Canada checked with their labor bureau, they were given the address of the farm "Norman" was working at.

The police had also received a small piece of paper that was literally a "message in a bottle." A woman found the bottle with the note rolled up inside on the banks of the Columbia River. The typed written note read:

Whoever discovers this bottle will do me a great favor if they will notify my friends that I was not in Redmond at all, and further, I was not the hobo that rode on the blind baggage as the newspapers have it. I am a slicker and these guys will never get me because they are too damned slow to catch cold. I will be in St. Paul at the Hotel Ryan on the 21st of July and from there I am going to Buenos Aires. Cordially yours, R.M. Brumfield.[5]

Although Melvin was not willing to tell a reporter from the *Portland Telegram* anything about the crime, he did talk about his journey from Oregon to Canada. He said he had read about the case in newspapers. He told the reporter:

When night came on the evening of July 13th, I started from Roseburg and walked to Oakland [Oregon.] I waited around Oakland until train time and then I rode on into Portland and stayed there for several hours. I decided to keep on going north and rode right through to Seattle. I stayed around there for a day and decided to cross into Canada. I arrived in Vancouver the next day and lay around there for another two days. I then decided to go to Alberta, so I got on a train and rode to Lake Louise, where I again stopped for several days. At each place I stopped I secured newspapers and read of my escape.

... From Lake Louise I went to Banff and Calgary. I applied for work at a labor bureau here, giving the name of Norman Whitney. Unable to get work at that time, I waited around for a couple of days and was then directed to Vadar's farm at Midnapore."[6]

When asked, "Who are you supposed to have murdered?" Melvin quickly responded, "I do not have to tell you that. I don't want to say anything about it."

When asked if he was going to fight extradition, Melvin said, "I am willing to waive extradition and go back to Roseburg tonight. I will tell District Attorney Neuner everything I know."

Back in Roseburg, Mrs. Brumfield refused to believe her husband had been located in Canada. She simply stated, "It is not true." A reporter later told her that Melvin had said, "Send my love to my wife and three children and tell them that everything will be all right."

Once Mrs. Brumfield received the message, she told a reporter: "I have always had the utmost faith in my husband and I know everything will come out all right. I am so glad that he has sent that message and I want to thank him sincerely for communicating it to me."

Melvin soon found himself back in the United States facing a charge of murder in the first degree. He was arraigned and ordered to be held without bail. A grand jury indicted Melvin of murder in the first degree. Melvin's defense attorneys Dexter Rice and A. N. Orcutt requested a three-week delay due to the volume of documents that they had to wade through and the fact that many witnesses were in Canada. They added there would be a shortage of jurors available due to the prune harvest taking place. Judge Bingham was quick to reply: "I have observed that about this time of the year, a man who owns a prune orchard thinks the whole world revolves around that orchard."

District Attorney Neuner gave his opinion that three weeks would be too long to delay the trial. Judge Bingham granted their request and stated that the trial would begin in three weeks. Next the defense attorneys argued for a change in venue. District Attorney Neuner stated that newspapers throughout the state of Oregon had followed the story. He argued that there was not a county in the entire state that would be more or less impartial than Douglas County. Witnesses were called to the stand to give their opinion on the matter. Finally, Judge Bingham denied the change in venue request, saying it was not necessary. He did concede that due to the publicity of the case, it might take a while to seat a jury.

If the citizens of Roseburg thought the crowds were large for the coroner's inquest, they were in for a shock when Melvin's trial got underway. The entire town was packed with people wanting to know firsthand what was happening inside the courthouse.

Special Prosecutor Hammersly told the jury that Melvin had used Dennis as a pawn to escape his life, which was fraught with the financial woes that he had brought on himself. Special Prosecutor Hammersly told the members of the jury that Melvin chose Dennis because of a similar body type, height, and weight, and because Dennis lived as a hermit, he would not be missed if he were to disappear. The defense attorneys were claiming insanity on the part of their client.

Melvin took the witness stand and claimed he had no memory of anything that occurred from two days prior to the incident up until recently. Without offering an explanation, he stated there were two exceptions to this—one while he was in Portland, the other time when he was in Victoria, British Columbia.

The prosecution showed Melvin a letter the Canadian police had found in his room at the ranch in Calgary. The contents of the letter indicated that Dennis was alive and it was he who was deceased. The letter was signed Dennis Russell. Melvin admitted on the witness stand that the handwriting was his, but he had no recollection of having written the letter.

Sheriff Starmer testified that when he and Deputy Sheriff Webb arrived at the jail in Canada, Melvin claimed to be Dennis Russell. Sheriff Starmer did not miss a beat and said, "Sure, you're Dennis Russell, you're just the man we want. You're wanted for murder down in Roseburg." The sheriff said that during the train ride from Canada to Oregon, Melvin mentioned his memory loss. However, at one point, Melvin inquired if his automobile had sustained heavy damage. Another time he asked if his gun was destroyed. When informed his gun had been burned in the explosion, he said nothing and just stared out the window.

Drs. Stewart and Houck spoke of completing a *post mortem* examination on the deceased. They discovered the body had sustained two bullet wounds. They went into detail about the impact of the dynamite on the body.

A report was introduced written by Dr. C. S. Mahood, medical officer of health of the city of Calgary, Canada. Dr. Mahood examined Melvin while he was in the jail in Calgary. In his report, he wrote:

After apprehension and on examination after admission to the police cells here, Dr. Brumfield gave one the picture of a person in a very dejected condition. He appeared apathetic, unkempt and sickly. There was a very faraway look on his face which gave evidence of mental deterioration with little if any affection and mannerism. He complained of violent headache, dizziness and inability to sleep. His appetite and digestion were impaired and he suffered from intestinal toxemia. If disturbed in his cell, he became intensely irritable restless, depressed and anxious. He showed evidence of developing hallucinations and delusion of an inconstant and instable nature and of short duration.

He appeared dazed, perplexed and was not to concentrate his mind on anything but the cry that "Doc was killed."[7]

"He denied he was Dr. Brumfield, and that 'Doc' was killed in an automobile accident. He had a childish, affected, inconsequential way of answering questions, which showed both intelligence and understanding impaired. Persons in the condition in which the doctor appeared here have been known to commit various senseless and most peculiar acts. He showed a marked emotional defect and seemed to care nothing for friends or family. He appeared to realize something was the matter and to me he seemed to fear insanity. All of his actions and mental processes while here were remarkable slow."

Walter Bowman testified to seeing a car alongside the road that appeared to have a man's legs dangling out the window. The driver suddenly drove onto the highway, but in doing so, seemed to zigzag across the road before straightening out.

Financial documents were introduced showing Melvin's total indebtedness to be $26,200. The total of Melvin's insurance policies was $27,000. The prosecution maintained that the dentist faked his own death with the thought of starting over in a foreign land. The district attorney showed a letter written by Melvin to a Canadian steamship company requesting information on passports and sailing dates for Australia.

On the morning of October 14, 1921, the buzz in the courthouse was enough to drone out the sound of the hail outside. All eyes were on Mrs. Clara Killio, a chambermaid Melvin had met at Lake Louise. Clara took the stand and said she had met the man she knew as Norman Whitney the previous July while she was working at the Chateau-Lake Louise. She said he told her he planned to sail to Australia on September 10, 1921. She said he left the Chateau on August 2, 1921, and sent her one letter that was not introduced into evidence. Rumors had been circulating prior to Clara's testimony that Melvin left his family to start a new life with Clara. However, the prosecution was never able to determine that he knew Clara prior to meeting her when he stayed at the Chateau.

There was much speculation about the now infamous pink skirt sold to a woman in the Burchard General Store at the time Melvin came into the store wanting a box. The box that Melvin tried to ship to Banff was introduced. The local newspaper reported that the spectators in the courtroom stopped swatting at flies long enough to crane their necks to get a glimpse of the box that had been Melvin's undoing. Within the confines of the cardboard box was the pink skirt. Melvin smiled when the skirt was held up. He was still smiling when articles of woman's undergarments were pulled out of the box along with miscellaneous items from the store. Mrs. Burchard took the witness stand and identified each item, even the Christmas decorations that she kept in the box, in the back of the store. She explained that the books in the box had the name "Norman Whitney" because that was the name of her nephew. Mrs. Burchard told the jury how Melvin had nodded to the lady purchasing the skirt when he came in to request a box.

Neither the prosecution nor the defense could offer an explanation as to how the pink skirt got in the box or why it was to be shipped to Banff. Some of the crowd thought Melvin knew Clara ahead of time and that he had purchased the skirt for her. Her employer verified that she had never left Banff during her almost two-year employment. Others thought the skirt was evidence that Mrs. Brumfield was in on the entire scam and she planned to join her husband in another country. There were others, though, that believed Melvin was planning on disguising himself as a female when he sailed to Australia.

Most of the witnesses were the same as those who had testified at the coroner's inquest or the grand jury. However, this time, the defense called Dr. B. F. Scacfe to the stand. He testified that Melvin was "insane and homicidally dangerous." He further stated that Melvin was insane on the day of the incident. Dr. Scacfe noted Melvin's "depression, pains about the eyes, his failure to remember and his habit of pacing the floor, indicated insanity." The prosecution wasted no time in putting Dr. William House on the stand, who emphatically stated that Melvin was indeed sane based on his findings after speaking to him in his jail cell. J. W. Perkins, his business landlord, testified that there were no signs of insanity anytime he dealt with Melvin. Dr. Fred Haynes, a fellow dentist, said the same thing.

Finally, it was time for the prosecution and the defense to put the case into the juror's hands. Judge Bingham read their instructions and explained their options in finding the defendant guilty or innocent.

As the jury filed out to begin deliberations, Melvin was led back to his cell by the guards. He was allowed a moment to speak to his wife. He advised her to go home and get some rest. Once back in his cell, he suggested to his cellmates that they play some cards. He sat down at the table and began dealing the cards. He continued playing cards with his cellmates, oblivious to the fact that at that moment, twelve people were deciding if he would live or die.

Outside the courthouse, crowds gathered on the lawn. Some people had been at the courthouse since early morning; others who had worked all day arrived in the evening. Finally, it was time; the jury had returned. The guards came to collect Melvin. As they led him to the courthouse, it began to rain—perhaps a sign of things to come.

At seventeen minutes to midnight, the twelve jurors filed into the courtroom. It had taken them just over three hours to deliberate, but they had reached a verdict. Foreman W. E. Clingenpeel handed the piece of paper to the bailiff, who, in turn, handed it to Judge Bingham. The judge glanced at the paper for a moment, then passed it to Clerk Riddle and asked him to read the verdict. "Guilty of first-degree murder as charges in the indictments" were the words spoken by Clerk Riddle.

The "Extra" edition of *The News-Review* published in the hours after the verdict reported on the scene in the courtroom. They told how Melvin slumped in his seat, and beads of sweat appeared on his forehead. They said Mrs. Brumfield entered the courthouse moments after the verdict was read. She spoke to him and smiled, unaware that the verdict had been read. The reporter described Melvin was "like a statue" and did not notice his wife had entered the room. *The News-Review* reported:

> A ray of hope was still shining in the face of the woman who had held up so bravely during the fearful ordeal of the last two weeks. The eyes of everyone in the courtroom were upon the couple and then Brumfield gathered himself together, leaned towards his wife and said two words: "First degree.[8]

Mrs. Brumfield immediately slipped into her chair, her eyes at first brimming with tears, but soon, she was sobbing uncontrollably. Judge Bingham dismissed the jury and stated he would pronounce the sentence on Saturday morning at 9 a.m.

A guard appeared on each side of Melvin and began walking him back to his cell. At one point, he stopped for a moment and asked, "So that's the verdict, is it?" One of the guards nodded and they continued on. As they entered the jail, his cellmates looked up expectedly. Melvin walked past them, took off his coat, and simply said, "First degree, boys."

One of his cellmates repeated, "First degree?" "Yep" was all that Melvin had to say. His cellmates were moved to another cell as was the policy for a convicted murderer. Melvin's cell was searched by the guards for anything he could use to harm himself. Before he went to sleep, Sheriff Starmer asked, "Anything you want, Doc?"

Melvin replied, "No, Sam, I'm fixed all right."

The next morning, Melvin was sound asleep when Sheriff Starmer asked him if he had anything to say to the newspaper reporters. The answer came quickly, "I am innocent. Even if the whole world condemns me, in the eyes of God I am innocent, but I am not afraid to meet death." When a reporter asked if he was surprised by the verdict, Melvin answered:

> Well, I will tell you. I am just as innocent of that as anybody could be, but I wasn't surprised at the verdict, because I wasn't able to help my lawyers, and the evidence was as damning as could be, but just as sure as there is a God in heaven, I am innocent. If I thought for one minute that I was responsible for that man's death, I would have said so. I say now, I am innocent, and I will always say I am innocent. I am not afraid to die for this thing, but that doesn't make me guilty. I know the story I told sounded like an awful wild one, but they are the only facts I know.[9]

All that remained was for Judge Bingham to pronounce Melvin's sentence, but before that could happen, there was more drama in the case. Melvin was found in his jail cell, barely alive, having attempted to commit suicide by slashing his neck. Whether he used a razor or a piece of his own dental work was never determined. What was determined, though, was he as not shot in the neck the night before while at the post office as he claimed. Upon learning of the new development, Judge Bingham told the court, "I cannot sentence a half-dead man."

On the morning of Halloween 1921, Melvin was brought into court. Judge Bingham pronounced, "You have been convicted of first-degree murder and it is the sentence of this court that on January 13th you hang by the neck until dead." This was the first time Judge Bingham had ever sent anyone to the gallows, and it was obvious to those in the courtroom that he was deeply troubled by having to do so. When the judge asked if he had anything to say, he calmly stated, "As God is my judge, I don't know how Dennis Russell met death." Mrs. Brumfield sat silently in the courtroom.

The next morning, large crowds gathered at the courthouse and at the train depot hoping to catch a glimpse of Melvin as he headed to the Oregon State Penitentiary. Sheriff Starmer, who had been there since day one, was on hand to finish the task. He was accompanied by Deputy Daugherty and a reporter, Bert Bates, from *The News-Review* out of Roseburg. Melvin appeared to be very weak and lacked the grandeur he had exhibited the last time he and Sheriff Starmer were at the train depot—on their return from Canada.

As the train made its way to Salem, crowds gathered at train depots along the way in the hopes of seeing the man they had read so much about. Along the journey, Melvin asked Deputy Daugherty to contact Reverend Spencer to see if he would be willing to visit him at the prison. A few hours into the trip, Melvin told Sheriff Starmer, "I am getting tired Sam. I hope we arrive soon."

When they arrived at the train depot in Salem, the crowds were so large that the local police had to hold people back as they attempted to get close enough to see Melvin. The prisoner was flanked by prison guards who escorted him to the prison automobile for the final leg of their journey. When they arrived at the prison, they encountered a small crowd waiting by the gate. Melvin was taken into the receiving portion of the prison. He was taken to his new home, cell 117 on death row—a far cry from his luxurious home in Roseburg. Sheriff Starmer and Deputy Daugherty shook hands with the prisoner and Sheriff Starmer said, "Good-bye, Doc."

Melvin became emotional but managed to quickly say, "Good-bye boys."

Deputy Warden Lewis went over the rules of the prison with his new charge and told him, "We will expect you to follow all of our rules and conduct yourself as a model prisoner."

Melvin readily agreed to this by saying, "I will be a model prisoner, warden, and observe all of your rules closely. I can assure you that I will cause you no trouble."

Within weeks, Melvin's defense attorneys filed a 102-page appeal along with a transcript that numbered 500 pages. At contention was that Special Prosecutor Hammersley had no jurisdiction to prosecute the case, that a change in venue should have been granted, and that the grand jury was not properly empaneled.

While they were waiting for the appeal to be heard, the entire death penalty was being re-examined in Oregon. A few months later, the Oregon Supreme Court ruled that the death penalty could continue to be used for first-degree murder cases.

In July 1922, the Oregon Supreme Court ruled against allowing Melvin to be granted a new trial. His attorneys then asked the Oregon Supreme Court for a rehearing based on their belief that they did not take the time to fully study the case before denying a new trial. Before a decision could be made, Melvin made his own decision.

"Under the circumstances life is not worth living." Those were the opening words in a suicide letter addressed to Warden Lewis. Melvin committed suicide on September 13, 1922. A guard found him in his cell where he had hanged himself by using a bedsheet. He had rolled his blanket up so it appeared that the bed was occupied during bed checks throughout the night. In his letter to the warden, he stated many points of contention about his jury trial. It was his belief that he did not get a fair trial and that the jury had missed numerous points that would have set him free. He ended the letter saying, "You have treated me fine here. You are real men. I hope I have not been too much trouble."

Melvin also wrote a letter to his wife. The first sentence read, "I hope you are not terribly shocked by my determination to go on over." He spoke of his love for her and thanked her for sticking by him. He emphasized his innocence in Dennis' death.

A small service was held at the Portland Crematorium. A total of seven people were in attendance, but Mrs. Brumfield and their three boys were not present. Two small floral arrangements rested by the vault.

11

The Murdered Accountant

On the morning of November 20, 1933, Imo Akin was in a hurry to get to her job as a school teacher at Shattuck Grammar School. Just before 8 a.m., she dashed out of the apartment she shared with her husband, Frank, in Portland, saying she would be home later that afternoon.

Mrs. C. E. King was sleeping in her apartment directly below the Akins' home when she heard a gunshot and the sound of something heavy hitting the floor sometime before 9 a.m. She figured the gunshot was somewhere outside and fell back to sleep.

Leo Hartoin was working as the manager at the Akins' apartment. One of his duties was to let cleaning personnel and repairmen into the apartments in his building. When the Akins' housekeeper arrived at 9:30 a.m., he accompanied her to the Akins' apartment and unlocked the door so she could begin her work. As soon as he opened the door, he saw Frank lying dead from an apparent gunshot wound. He immediately called the Portland Police Bureau.

W. Frank Akin was a forty-three-year-old accountant. He had recently been appointed by Oregon Governor Julius Meier to audit the books of the Port of Portland. As a special agent to Governor Meier, he was to investigate any wrongdoings at the Port of Portland and report back to the governor. Frank had recently completed his assignment and given Governor Meier an 1,800-page report listing all of the irregularities he had uncovered. The Port of Portland was a very integral part of the city's business success. They oversaw the airport, as well as all imports and exports that came through the Port of Portland.

The investigators that arrived at the crime scene quickly determined that Frank had been shot with a small caliber revolver. They could tell immediately the wound was not self-inflicted.

Governor Meier was shocked by the news and immediately asked Oregon State Police Superintendent Charles Pray to report to his office. Superintendent Pray promised that his agency would work closely with the Multnomah County Sheriff's Office and the Portland Police Bureau.

The governor was concerned that the investigation Frank had just completed for him regarding the Port of Portland had cost him his life. Within the documents that Frank had provided him, he listed port manager, James H. Polhemus, Commissioner Kenneth W. Dawson, and retiring chairman Frank M. Warren with practices that were "against the best interests of the commission and the public."

The report had been presented to three members of the port commission—Bert Haney, Paul Bates, and Frank Warren. Hearings had been held for three weeks giving the employees listed in the report a chance to explain their side. At the end of the hearings, Bert and Paul called for the resignation of Polhemus along with other key employees. Frank Warren submitted his own report stating that the charges were unfounded or the charges had been explained satisfactorily. Frank was due to appear before the special session of the legislature the morning he was killed.

At the crime scene, detectives believed Frank had known his killer and had invited him into the apartment. The security chain was not broken as though someone had forced their way in. The apartment was not in disarray. Frank's gun was in a drawer in a table and his wallet had not been touched. The apartment manager told the police the security chain was not in place when he let the housekeeper in. The body was located several steps from the doorway.

Later, when Dr. Warren Hunter performed an autopsy, he reported that Frank died almost instantly, therefore he had not been able to move very far from where he was shot. When the police interviewed the neighbors, one woman said she let a man into the building that morning at about 8:30 a.m. She saw him fumbling for keys and assumed he lived in the building. The only description she had was that he was about 6 feet tall, heavyset, and middle-aged. He wore a hat and overcoat.

One name that came up early on as a possible suspect was Stewart Yoeman. Governor Meier recalled that Yoeman had shown up at Frank's apartment holding a gun and threatening to shoot him. He was able to calm Yoeman down and he later chose not to press charges. Within hours of the murder, Stewart found himself at a police station being questioned, but he was released when the officers were confident that he was not involved.

Over the next several days, many of Frank's business associates were questioned by the police. Frank's assistant, Louise Ellensberger, went over Frank's schedule with the investigators. Mark Israel, a local pawnbroker and jeweler, came forward with information. According to Mark, Frank had had an affair with a woman who had begun threatening him to the point that he carried a loaded gun. He told the detectives that Frank had confessed the affair to his wife. Gladys Johnson was soon seated across from police detectives. She admitted to being angry at Frank a few years before after Frank invested some money for her from a divorce settlement. It turned out to be a bad investment and Gladys lost all of her money. She stressed to the detectives she blamed Frank, but never threatened him with death.

The investigators learned that Frank had real estate investments. Additionally, he was the main investor of Akin Butte Oil Company. The oil company was based in Wyoming and was intended to make money for investors by drilling for oil. The investors ended up losing their money when the well failed to produce oil.

Investigators spoke with port manager Polhemus, who told them he received a phone call the morning of Frank's murder wherein the caller said, "Well, I see you got your man." He also told the police that someone fired a weapon through a window in his home two weeks prior to Frank's murder, but he did report the incident at the time.

Within a short time, a bill was introduced in the House of Representatives that was meant to end racketeering and prohibit threatening public officials and investigators of law and crime. The bill also allowed for rewards of up to $1,000 if it could be proven that a murder took place to cover up a crime or to prevent prosecution. Once the bill was passed, the port of Portland offered a $1,000 reward for information leading to the arrest and conviction of Frank's killer.

Within the first six weeks of the investigation, law enforcement officials interviewed almost 100 people but they were completely stumped. The Multnomah County Sheriff's Office pulled their investigators from the case, citing that they were needed elsewhere. A coroner's inquest was conducted and nineteen witnesses took the stand. Not one of the witnesses was able to shed any light on the investigation. In the end, they returned a verdict stating Frank was killed by an unidentified person.

The Port of Portland commission rejected Frank Akin's report and instead voted 6-3 in favor of Frank Warren's report. His report absolved all employees from any wrongdoing.

The Multnomah County Grand Jury began studying the case in May 1934. District Attorney Langley told the media that due to the volume of the evidence presented, they would work on it when they were not occupied by other cases. At the end of the year, they adjourned, having reached no conclusion.

Eighteen months after Frank's murder, the police in Washington state responded to a cottage in Erland's Point near Bremerton, where they found six people who had been brutally murdered. The victims were Frank Flieder age fifty; his wife, Anna, age fifty; Eugene Chenevert; his wife, Peggy, age thirty; Magnus Jordan, age fifty; and Fred Balsom. The investigators could tell that a tremendous struggle had taken place, and they believed one or more of the suspects was injured based on blood left behind that did not match any of the victims.

The Washington case was stalled until Peggy Paulos decided to tell the police everything she knew. She offered details about the Bremerton murders. She told the investigators Leo Hall had overheard Mrs. Flieder saying she had a large sum of money at her cottage. Leo convinced Peggy to accompany him to the cottage. The two were acquainted from the time Peggy's husband was in prison. Peggy admitted to the investigators that she did go to the cottage with Leo. She gave details about the murders, which involved the use of a gun, a hammer, a carving knife, a stove poker, and a blackjack, leaving six people dead.

Peggy also implicated Leo in Frank's murder. She told the detectives she was not present for that murder, but she had spoken to Leo about it before and after it occurred. It was her belief that Leo was paid $1,200 to kill Frank. Peggy was charged with the murder for the Washington case, to which she pled not guilty.

As the investigators in two states worked to piece all of this together, they determined that Jack Justice hired Larry Paulos to knock on Frank's door and threaten him with a gun months before he was killed. It was Larry's statement that Jack told him a lady who had lost a great deal of money hired him to kill Frank. Their investigation revealed that Jack hired Leo to kill Frank.

Leo was formally charged with Frank's murder. At the time, he was still in Washington. The police there arrested him on a weapons charge and were questioning him about the Bremerton murders. At first, he gave a false name but eventually admitted to his true identity. The police also asked him about the murder of Frank, but he was not talking about either case.

At Leo's arraignment on the Washington case, witnesses told of his plan to rob a department store and to kidnap the children of a prominent family. Details were given about a robbery that Leo reportedly committed where a male was hit over the head with a hammer. Walter Butterfield testified, "Hall told me there was a man in Portland who was 'doing a little political work' and that we could get a thousand dollars to 'rub him out.'"

Two months later, the trial got underway in Washington for Peggy and Leo, who were tried together. The jury was taken to the cottage to get a feel for the layout. They were shown photographs from the crime scene, causing one juror to faint. Peggy testified that Leo had planned to rob the six people, thinking they would all have money and jewelry. She told the jurors that Leo told her one of the six people recognized him and he decided to not leave any witnesses. Three witnesses testified to seeing Leo the day after the murders, with a fresh scar on his face. A nurse was called to testify that Dr. McWhinnie stitched Leo's face using a total of twenty-four stitches. Leo's mother and brothers provided an alibi for him. The jury did not believe the alibi and convicted him. He was sentenced to hanging. Peggy was acquitted and walked free, although she was the recipient of so many death threats that she went into hiding.

Jack Justice was charged with hiring Leo to murder Frank. A trial got underway in Portland in 1936. The jury's first task at hand was to visit the apartment where the murder had taken place. The defense took the stance that Gladys hired someone to kill Frank because she was upset about losing her investment money. Jack took the stand in his own defense. He denied hiring Leo to kill Frank.

The jury returned a verdict of guilty and recommended life in prison for Jack. Leo was indicted for Frank's murder but before he could be tried, he lost his appeal in the Washington case and was hanged at the prison in Walla Walla. When asked if he had any final words at his execution, Leo stated, "I would like to say the Justice they convicted in the Akin case was an entirely innocent man. Jack Justice never hired me, or anyone else to kill Frank Akin. The charge they convicted him on was a bum charge."

Jack's attorney filed a request that the state furnish a transcript of the testimony from his trial for their appeal to the supreme court. The request was denied due to the cost being estimated at $1,000. The following year, the Oregon Supreme Court upheld Jack's conviction.

12

Edward Hugh Martin

On May 2, 1908, newspapers across Oregon blasted the news:

> The two men, who so fiendishly murdered and then mutilated the body
> of pawnbroker Nathan Wolff at six o'clock Friday evening at his store
> on First Street and then rifled the safe of about $1500, were Portland
> men and well known to their victim, is the present theory of Chief of
> Police Gritmacher and Captain of Detectives Bailey. Practically every
> plain clothes man in the Portland police force is out on the case today.
> A large force of regular officers have been brought in from their outside
> beats and detailed on the case. The police are shadowing two men, local
> thugs, who are suspected of knowing something of the dastardly work,
> if not actually implicated in the murder itself.[1]

Within a couple of blocks of the crime scene, the police found a man's
shirt that was torn and had a large blood stain on it. The shirt had been
discarded near a lodging house on Second Street. The shirt had a laundry
mark inside the collar. The police needed to tie the mark "A163" to the
owner of the shirt. They visited numerous laundries, but no one was able
to help them. Then at the Opera House Laundry, the owner was able to
tell them who the shirt belonged to.

Just when they thought they had their man, the suspect told them he
had sold a batch of shirts to Max Drey, who operated a second-hand
business. When they found Mr. Drey, he immediately recognized the shirt
as one that he had sold recently. He recalled the man purchased a total

of three shirts in one transaction the week before. He did not know the man's name, but he remembered the transaction took place outside of Solomon's Jewelry Store on Third Street. He told the investigators the man asked him if he wanted to make some quick cash. When he answered in the affirmative, the man mentioned he knew where there was a lot of cash and diamonds they could steal. At that time, Mr. Drey told the man he did not want anything to do the plan, which upset the man.

Police Captain Baty visited Solomon's Jewelry Store and spoke with the owner, Mr. Solomon. He recalled the transaction because it was between two parties that he knew. He said a man he was familiar with, Edward Martin, was in his store on April 24 and pawned a draughtmen's instrument. He had just paid Edward $5 for the tool, when Mr. Drey entered the store wanting to sell several shirts. Mr. Solomon told Mr. Drey he was not interested in purchasing the shirts. Edward overheard the conversation and asked Mr. Drey to wait for him outside.

Mr. Solomon told Captain Baty that Edward had pawned jewelry at his store about a dozen times in the past. He said that sometimes he used the alias "S. A. Sutton," but always listed the same home address. He said Edward usually came in to the store in the evenings. Mr. Solomon told the police he was convinced Edward was a "dangerous man" based on his actions and his demeanor. He mentioned that Edward had to win every argument. Mr. Solomon said he was convinced Edward was using cocaine or another drug based on his observations. He summed up his beliefs by saying Edward was a "dope fiend."

The police initially believed there were two men involved in the murder, but as they learned more about Edward, they came to the conclusion that he acted alone. A warrant was issued for the arrest of Edward Hugh Martin for the murder of Nathan Wolff.

Many business owners donated money for a reward for the capture of the murderer. Additionally, Judge Webster and County Commissioners Lightner and Barnes authorized spending $1,000 for a reward to be paid out upon the conviction of the person responsible for killing Nathan.

Now that the police knew the name of their suspect, they began an earnest search for him, but it was not going to be easy. As the police searched for Edward, they learned he was far from your typical criminal. Edward was raised in New York and lived a privileged life with his wealthy family. Edward served in the Spanish–American War. He earned two life-saving medals after saving six people from drowning. He graduated from West Point in 1898. He was also a graduate of Fordham College and the New York Law School. While in New York, he was engaged to Katherine Travers, who was from a prominent family. The engagement was broken off, allegedly due to his speculating in the stock market.

While serving as a second lieutenant in the United States Army in 1900, Edward was charged with forging three documents at the canteen. He was court martialed. Before his trial was over, rumors began circulating that he had married a young lady by the name of Grace "Gussie" McKee. She had been in trouble with the law herself. She ran a pool hall and when questioned by the police she was using two different aliases. The charges against her were conducting a pool hall for women. Eventually, her case was dismissed, but Edward was found guilty. During the court martial, it was proven that Edward forged three documents. This led to President McKinley issuing Edward a dishonorable discharge from the United States Army.

Edward then turned to passing bad checks signed by army officials. In one instance, he showed the merchant his ring from West Point in an effort to legitimize who he was and that the check was signed by a military official. The fraudulent checks led to Edward serving one year in Sing Sing prison.

It was not long after he was released that he was back in handcuffs. Edward was arrested on burglary charges after he was located next to a drug store that had just been burglarized. The owner of the drug store had been asleep in the back room when he was awoken by a burglar at 3 a.m. Edward was located in the hallway next to the business. He claimed he was intoxicated and could not remember being in the store. A handkerchief was found in the store with the letter "M" on it. Charges of burglary were dismissed when the owner of a drug store could not identify him. His father was in the courtroom and promised to look after his son. By that time, it was known that Edward was using morphine and his behavior was becoming more and more erratic.

Next Edward was picked up for vagrancy for being intoxicated at Bath Beach. At the time, he was a suspect in a burglary at a home in Bath Beach. Those charges were dropped as well.

When Edward first arrived in Oregon, he studied medicine at the University of Oregon for one year. Next, he began working as a temporary employee for the city of Portland's engineering office. He had not been on the job very long when he was arrested for possessing opium. The charges were dropped because he was a city employee.

The detectives learned that on the day of the murder, Edward found out that he had not been selected for a position with the city of Portland.

He learned that even though he had placed fourth in the civil service exam, he was not chosen for the city sealer of weights and measures. To add to that, he learned he had scored 98 percent in trigonometry and geometry but failed other parts of the civil service exam for a position in the city engineer's office. He tried to convince the city officials to change his score but was not successful in his endeavor.

Edward's wife, Gussie, died soon after they married. He re-married and he was sharing a home with his new wife. The police went to Edward's home to ask his wife about the shirt. She said when he came home at midnight on Friday, he was not wearing a shirt. In fact, he was wearing an overcoat and vest that she had never seen before. Edward's wife told the detectives that she and Edward went to church Sunday morning, but she had not seen him since Sunday evening. Detectives Jones and Tichenor spent the night outside Edward's home in the hope he would return.

Due to Edward's past as a war hero and West Point graduate, newspapers across the country carried the story. After reading the newspaper article, Chief of Police Secrist of Vancouver, Washington, contacted the Portland Police Bureau to inform them of his contact with Edward. According to Chief Secrist, Edward had been arrested in Vancouver the previous summer for robbing a pawnbroker. Chief Secrist explained that Edward had walked into a pawnshop, identified himself as a lieutenant in the United States Army, and asked the owner, Mr. Clow, about the price of a revolver. Edward managed to open the store safe and grabbed $15. Mr. Clow saw what happened and contacted the police. Edward became irate when Chief Secrist took him into custody, saying, "Officer do you know what you are doing when you arrest an officer of the United States Army?"

Once at police headquarters, the police located $15 in Edward's shoe. He was charged with grand larceny but the charges were dropped to petty larceny. Edward paid a $30 fine and was released from custody.

The investigators also learned that Edward had a sordid past in Idaho. After his prison stint in Sing Sing, Edward and a partner, Floyd Barrett, worked several mining claims in Idaho. The partnership was backed financially by investors from New York. In 1903, the men told the media they expected their claims to be one of the largest and most productive in the United States within five years. Yet before the five years were up, a man by the name of Mr. Kroll turned up missing, with Edward a suspect in the disappearance.

While working in the mines, Edward took on the moniker "Doc" for attending to people's injuries. Mr. Kroll was to meet Edward for the first time near the Belvidere Mine. The two were seen in town purchasing some meat at a butcher shop before riding their horses back to the mine. The following day, Edward brought Mr. Kroll's horse and pack outfit into town. He returned the meat they had purchased and received a refund. He headed to the area of Roosevelt and sold Mr. Kroll's horse and pack outfit. He also sold two watches.

By this time, a fire that had been burning for a while became significant enough to be seen a distance away. The fire was in the area that Edward and Mr. Kroll had camped the night before. Those in the mining industry believed Edward had murdered Mr. Kroll, set the logs on top of the body, and started a fire to cover up the murder scene. Mr. Kroll was never seen or heard from again. The law enforcement officials told the media, "We are not going to put the taxpayers of this county to the enormous expense of going into these isolated parts looking for evidence." A few months later, deputies did head into the forest in search of Mr. Kroll's body, but they were turned away by deep snow. That was their only attempt at locating the missing man.

Edward was arrested for larceny of a rifle and sentenced to six months in the Grangeville, Idaho, jail. A reporter from the *Lewiston Tribune* asked Edward about the disappearance of Mr. Kroll. Edward replied:

I do not believe Kroll is dead. He and Mrs. Burgdorf were the most bitter enemies I or any man could have, and it is through their own lies and deceitful maneuvers I am having to stand the persecution for that affair, about which I know nothing. As to having a watch said to have belonged to Kroll, I did have it, but I bought it from another man, paying him five dollars for it. There are several other points the state holds as evidence against me, but they are false statements made by my enemies, and I only hope they will find Kroll, for he is alive and well as far as I am concerned, and the search for him will be successful.[2]

Edward was released from jail, but not before trying to burn down the jail. Jailor Rambo discovered Edward had set his bed on fire. The jailor got that fire out, but within the hour, he set some papers on fire.

Not one to go quietly, Edward made such a scene on the train at Lewiston that several of the passengers held him down until they could turn him over to the sheriff. Those who had contact with him on the train believed he was under the influence of drugs. He eventually made it to Oregon, bringing his problems with him.

The police continued their investigation into Edward's life. The investigators visited other pawnshops in Portland and learned Edward had pawned his West Point ring on several occasions. They also learned he had pawned a revolver on the day of the murder. Many of the pawnbrokers described Edward as being a difficult customer. They recalled times when he would insist on a particular price for an item he was pawning.

The police learned Edward stopped by a butcher shop where his wife's relative, James Boyle, worked. This was about 10 a.m. on Monday, three days after the murder. He then went to the Boyle's house where he spoke with Mrs. Boyles. She later told the police:

> He was terribly excited and the sweat was standing out on his face. I begged him to give himself up to the police, but he said he had already agreed to do so at five o'clock. He asked me to telephone my husband and find out when he would be home, and when I told him to do so he said, "Oh, I can't go out of the house, they are following me so closely. They would catch me in a minute." When I asked him if he had killed the man he said, "No, I am as innocent as your little child standing there. I know nothing whatever about the murder of Wolff."
>
> … Then he wanted to leave his overcoat here with me, but I would not let him. I was terribly agitated and wished to get him out of the house before they found him here. But I did go to a neighbor and telephone the police as he asked me to, saying that he would give himself up at five o'clock.[3]

The police stationed fifty officers in the area to be ready to grab Edward.

The police learned after Edward left the Boyles' house, he headed to the Venata rooming-house. He asked the landlady, Mrs. Ida Patges, if he could rent him a room for a short period of time, telling her, "I am tired." He paid her fifty cents for the use of the room and asked to see the latest edition of *The Oregon Daily Journal*. Edward read the newspaper and then went to a telephone and phoned his friend Carl Blakney to inquire if he knew how his wife was doing. He asked Carl to visit him and to bring along their friend, H. H. Pomeroy.

It was Carl who phoned the police and informed them of Edward's whereabouts. Carl then headed to the Venata rooming house to see his friend. He later told the police:

> As I passed Penney's Saloon, Martin stuck his head out of the window on the Morrison Street side and called out to me. He met me on the

stairs and his first question was, "How is my wife?" We sat down and talked for a while and he said that he was innocent of the crime.[4]

Detectives Jones, Tychner, Hellyer, and Tichenor rushed to the Venata rooming house and got their man. The newspapers reported:

> He was bundled downstairs, hurriedly, and escorted to the corner of Grand Avenue where the crowd gathered so quickly that it was with extreme difficulty that the arresting officers could force their way through the blockading throngs, which jostled, pulled and tugged to get a look at him. Low murmurings and threats of violence were heard in the crowd, but mob law took no definite form, and the police hurried their bewildered prisoner along Grand Avenue toward Burnside Street bridge with all speed. At the east approach of the bridge, the party was met by the patrol wagon, and Martin was taken to police headquarters as fast as the horses could run.[5]

Edward was brought to the police headquarters and placed in a jail cell. The detectives noticed he had an abrasion behind his ear and deep scratches on his face and neck, which all appeared to be fresh.

A reporter from the United Press was granted an interview once Edward settled into his jail cell. Edward immediately said:

> I am innocent. I never committed the crime. The charge is too awful—it is horrible. What will my wife think? I can prove an alibi. I can do it by the testimony of my wife. I was with her at the time of the murder. I received those wounds in the hand by the scratch of a cat. The wound in my forehead came as the result of an axe handle breaking while I was splitting kindling Sunday. Sunday evening, I quarreled with my wife, and for that reason I had been staying away from home. The shirt I bought at the pawnshop for rough work and threw it away after a single day's wear. I tell you I am innocent, as innocent as a babe in its mother's arms.[6]

Edward's wife visited him at the jail the first evening he was behind bars. She confidently told the police officer her husband would be found innocent and that she would never testify against him. When she tried to kiss her husband through the bars of the jail cell, the guard pulled her back and would not allow the kiss. She quietly told her husband to not say a word to the police and told him, "Your father's attorneys in New York are securing counsel for you."

Edward's wife sent numerous cablegrams to Edward's father, but there was no response. He was thought to be travelling in Europe. A family member did secure an attorney for Edward, but the attorney resigned early on, leaving Edward's fate in the hands of a court-appointed defense attorney.

Due to his drug usage, the police knew they had to be careful in questioning Edward, who was in obvious signs of drug withdrawal. They feared if he did confess or he denied killing Nathan, it was simply because of drug withdrawals. In the hours after his arrest, Edward began suffering from drug withdrawals. He pleaded with the jail guards to get him some cocaine. At one point, he began moaning and crying so loud that other inmates began begging the guards to give him some drugs.

The police continued their investigation. They located a blood-stained overcoat and a rifle in a vacant lot near the water front. Although Edward told the detectives he did not own an overcoat, one witness told the authorities that he had seen Edward wearing a coat that looked similar to the one found in the vacant lot. The executors of Nathan's estate told the detectives that a rifle was missing from the pawnshop.

The police spoke to the manager of the hotel near where the bloodied shirt was found. He confirmed Edward had not stayed at his hotel. Based on that, the police believed that Edward stepped into the alley behind the hotel and changed out of the shirt, figuring he would not be observed. As there were other articles of discarded clothing in the alley, the police figured Edward would assume no one would pay any attention to the shirt. The police confirmed that a man by the name of J. H. Barrett of Salem registered at the Imperial Hotel Sunday and at the Belvedere Hotel on Monday.

The police interviewed many people that had had contact with Edward. Dr. James Zan, who knew Edward when he was in medical school at the University of Oregon, said in part:

> I didn't at the time know that he was addicted to the use of drugs, but in light of present knowledge, I can remember he was always very nervous and had an unsteady eye. He had the ill-at-ease manner of morphine fiends, though not knowing his habit I thought little of it.[7]

Dr. C. H. Wheeler said, "I often noticed that he was exceptionally nervous and flighty. From what little chance I had for observation I should never have noticed anything out of the way with him."

Edward's priest, Father McDevitt, said:

If Edward H. Martin committed the brutal crime with which he is charged, he was undoubtedly insane. It may be that impelled by a terrible craving for drugs he was incited to maniacal fury by some action of the pawnbroker, and attacked him in a fit of insane rage.[8]

Father McDevitt said Edward had previously been treated for insanity at Salem. He explained:

After his treatment at Salem, Martin seemed to have recovered, and until he resumed the use of drugs just recently, he was a man of exemplary habits. He was one of my best parishioners, was kind, obliging, and a gentleman at all times. Except during his occasional lapses, when he would go on a drug-inspired debauch, Martin was always an intelligent talker. I have long known that he was irresponsible on these occasions when he succumbed to the irresistible longing for morphine or cocaine. His home relations were pleasant, but always marred by the fear of the drug horror.[9]

Mrs. Grub came forward and told the police she loaned her 32-caliber revolver to Edward the day of the murder. She told the police she had known Edward for some time and he was a regular visitor to her house. He told her he needed the gun because he was planning on going target shooting with friends. She handed over the gun and did not think much of it because he had told her that when he was at West Point, he excelled at target shooting. Once she read about his arrest, she became concerned that she would be implicated in the murder.

The police learned that Nathan's estate was worth $15,000. The estate consisted of jewelry, weapons, and other items in the pawnshop. Nathan left behind a wife who was forty-five-years old. The couple had four young children at the time of Nathan's death. The children were Aline, eleven years old; George, eight years old; Ruth, seven years old; and Jeanette, five years old.

District Attorney Manning spoke to Edward at length about his background. He told the district attorney that he was born and grew up in New York state, that his father worked in real estate, and his parents were currently traveling in Europe. Edward said he was appointed to West Point in 1894 and graduated in 1898. He was commissioned a second lieutenant and assigned to service with the Twenty-First United

States Infantry. During his service, he was a company commander in Cuba. While serving in the San Juan Campaign, he contracted yellow fever. It was there that he was given morphine for the first time.

Edward explained to District Attorney Manning that he married his wife in New York and they moved to Oregon a year prior to his arrest. He began studying medicine at the University of Oregon. His father sent a weekly allowance while he was a student.

District Attorney Manning then began asking questions relating to the murder. His first question was, "Where were you May 1st?"

Edward thought for a moment then said, "Well, I left home about 8:45 and got back about five minutes to six. I was about town and saw different people." When asked who he saw, Edward was only able to give one name—Judge Cameron. He told the district attorney that on Sunday, he went to church with his wife and then spent the night at the Imperial Hotel, registering under an alias name, J. H. Barrett.

The questioning turned to the pawnshop. "When did you first meet Nathan Wolff?"

Edward answered, "When I first came to Portland, I took a watch to him and pawned it." He explained that he had only been to the pawnshop twice; the last time was about two months prior. When asked which room he killed Nathan in, Edward said calmly, but loudly, "Mr. Manning, I did not kill Nathan Wolff."

District Attorney Manning informed him that he might as well confess, stating, "I've got you in a hole."

Edward calmly replied, "You haven't got me in any hole, and I'm telling everything I know just as it happened." When the district attorney began asking about the marks on Edward's face and neck, he explained them away by saying he was chopping wood the previous week and the hatchet slipped, striking him in the head. The other marks he explained were caused by the family cat.

While still suffering from withdrawal symptoms, Edward agreed to speak to a reporter with *The Oregon Daily Journal*. He continued to deny all charges against him and said he had an alibi. When asked about his drug habit, Edward freely admitted he was a drug addict who used morphine and cocaine. He told the reporter while he was serving in the Spanish–American War, he was fighting at San Juan Hill when he contracted yellow fever. Edward expanded on the subject:

> While suffering so severely that I could no longer endure the pain, one
> of the surgeons gave me morphine to ease me. That was the start. For

four years I did not take any other drug than morphine. Then I became so bad and took the drug in such large quantities that I had to take cocaine in addition to morphine to relieve the effects of morphine. Then came the downfall rapidly. I could not free myself from the habit. I went to sanitarium after sanitarium, but it always came out the same. There is no cure for the man who once becomes a dope fiend. I know that, and nobody can ever make me believe otherwise.[10]

Edward told the reporter that his father had been the head of the detective unit in New York City before retiring and going into real estate. He said his parents visited him and his wife in Portland the year before, but they were currently traveling in Europe.

The reporter would later write that Edward's sentences rambled on incoherently when asked about the night of the murder. He pointed out to Edward that he had been drinking whiskey and taking morphine and cocaine the night Nathan was murdered and asked if it was possible that he could have killed Nathan without being aware of it at the time. Edward replied, "No, I don't believe that I was ever in that condition." When the reporter pressed the issue, Edward said, "I cannot conceive that I committed the murder. I cannot conceive such a thing."

Nathan's wife and daughter identified the overcoat that was located in the vacant lot as having belonged to Nathan. Upon seeing the coat, Nathan's daughter, Aline, said, "That's papa's coat." Further, Edward Eubanks, who worked in a clothing store, identified the coat as Nathan's. He remembered it because it was a special order. He told the detectives Nathan had made the purchase several months ago.

When confronted with this new evidence, Edward simply stated, "I bought it from a peddler in front of the Portland Hotel four months ago. I can prove this fact."

The jail guards had to clear crowds each evening that converged on the jail. They became increasingly worried that a mob would try and get inside and harm Edward. The public sentiment was angry towards the man who allegedly murdered Nathan.

One witness that came forward was James West. He told the police he was working near Nathan's store the night of the murder. He happened to look into the window of the pawnshop and saw Nathan with a customer. The police brought James to the jail and he positively identified Edward as the man he saw.

Perhaps it was a sign of what was to come at the trial that on the day jury selection was to begin, the power was knocked out in parts of

Portland when a monkey broke loose from his owner and climbed wires that came in contact with the chain around his neck. Every streetcar that ran off the wires came to a halt, and the nearby homes and businesses went dark.

Finally, the day came, the jury was selected and the trial began with Judge Cleland presiding. The jurors included Henry Carl, I. W. Butler, R. E. Gibson, T. J. Burns, J. G. Bacher, Napoleon Davis, F. B. Harrington, P. A. McPherson, C. J. Sweet, G. L. Hibbard, Fred Hungerford, and E. Versteeg. Attorney John A. Jeffrey was the chief counsel for the defendant. Deputy District Attorney Fitzgerald was representing the prosecution.

One of the first orders of business was to clear the courtroom of those standing in the back. Judge Cleland told the crowd that if they could not find a seat, they would have to leave. This meant that only 100 people would be able to hear first-hand what was said at a trial that promised to be anything but dull.

The jury was taken to the crime scene to get a feel for the layout. Once they returned to the courthouse, they listened to the testimony of the police officers who were the first to arrive at the scene of the crime. They described finding Nathan dead from being shot in the neck and then brutally attacked with an ax and the stock of a rifle. Also, among the first witnesses were two people who testified they had seen Edward wearing a coat that looked similar to the blood-stained coat that the prosecution presented. The prosecution introduced the blood-stained shirt as well as a blood-stained handkerchief and necktie recovered from the crime scene.

Edward's wife and sister-in-law attended court every day. They were there when the gun was introduced that the police had found along with the overcoat in a vacant lot. A witness by the name of J. F. Ewing testified that he had pawned the gun at Nathan's pawnshop at the end of March. He received $7 for it and was making payments of seventy-five cents per month. Police Officer Stark Lytle testified about being dispatched to the corner of Water and Montgomery after citizens found the coat and gun in a vacant lot. The defense claimed the blood-stained overcoat and gun the police located in the vacant lot had been planted to make their client look guilty. The prosecution explained to the jury that the gun in question was not the murder weapon, but it had been stolen from the pawnshop after the murder was committed.

Dr. Fred Ziegler was called to the stand. He had examined Edward's injuries the day of his arrest. He testified that the injuries could not have been caused by a cat. Edward, he explained, had deep wounds on his face, neck, and hands. Although Edward told the doctor he had injured his head while chopping wood, the doctor told the jury that the wounds did not align with that explanation. Dr. Ziegler spoke of being called to the crime scene and the brutality the victim endured. He said there were twenty wounds on the body, mainly on the head and face. There were cuts on the victim's skull and face. Additionally, the victim had been shot in the neck. Dr. Ziegler told the jury that the gunshot wound would not have been fatal. At that point in the trial, the prosecution introduced into evidence the ax that had been left at the crime scene.

Throughout the trial, Edward glanced around the courtroom, as though trying to get a feel for what the spectators were thinking. From time to time, he exchanged glances with his defense team and whispered to one of them.

Night watchman J. D. Robinson testified about noticing things amiss at the pawnshop on his nightly rounds. He told the jury he had known Nathan for ten years. When he noticed that the lights were not on at the pawnshop, he walked across the street to the nearest phone box and called the Wolff residence. Mrs. Wolff was alarmed because she assumed her husband was still at work. J. D. went back across the street and entered the store through an unlocked door and discovered Nathan's body.

The hotel clerk, W. W. Webb, from the Belvedere Hotel testified that Edward stayed at the hotel using the alias of J. H. Barrett. After the guest left, the hotel staff discovered a suitcase had been left behind in the room. They put the suitcase in the office, figuring someone would come for it. After reading that Edward used the alias of J. H. Barrett, they opened the suitcase. Among the many items of clothing were a pair of Dents gloves. Mrs. Wolff testified that the gloves belonged to her husband. She was able to tell the jurors the area of the gloves she had mended. The prosecution introduced the spool of thread she used to mend the gloves, which matched the thread on the gloves.

Those who had jockeyed for a seat in the courtroom the day Edward took the stand were extremely happy to be there. The two people who were not there were Mrs. Martin and her sister. It was the first time they had missed a day of testimony. Edward began his testimony by telling the jury he was innocent of the charges. The alibi that he had promised came in the way of saying he had fallen asleep in the barn on his property due to the amount of morphine and cocaine he had consumed. He admitted to borrowing a gun from Mrs. Grub the morning Nathan was killed, but said he sold it later that day. He further stated he had sold his own gun that day as well. His explanation for the sales was he needed to bring money home to his wife, who believed he was still working for the city of Portland, when in fact, he had been fired a month prior. He admitted he bought one shirt from Mr. Drey for thirty cents. Edward assured the jury that the overcoat they examined was his own, not Mr. Wolff's. Edward did admit to lying about the injuries to his face. He told the jurors that in fact his cat was not responsible. He explained that he had been in a bar brawl the night before the murder and had sustained the injuries at that time.

On the day of closing arguments, the jurors listened to Mr. Jeffrey for more than two hours as he attempted to convince them of his client's innocence. Again and again, he pinned the blame on the police for deciding early on that Edward was responsible and refusing to look at any evidence that did not support that early theory. He referred to the coat and gloves and said they had been hidden by a fairy and then identified Detective Tichenor as that fairy. He referred to the blood-stained shirt as worthless evidence. Mr. Jeffrey reminded the jury that it had never been proven that the red stains on the overcoat were indeed blood, saying the stains could be from paint or blackberry juice. Mr. Jeffrey tried to discredit the statements that Mr. Drey made. He summed up the prosecutor's case by saying it was, "too flimsy and miserable to use even in a petty larceny case." He asked the jury to acquit his client so that they would never have to live with the regret of sending an innocent man to his death.

Deputy District Attorney Fitzgerald addressed the jury by saying, "Here we have Dr. Jekyll Martin. The man who studied at the university, went to West Point, and fought for his country." Then pointing a finger at the defendant, he said, "And here, we have Mr. Hyde Martin, the morphine fiend and blood-soaked assassin." He described the defense theories as "hop dreams." He asked the jury to return a guilty verdict in order to keep the public safe from those, "who shoot others down in cold blood to rob and to pillage."

After nine days of testimony, the jury began deliberations. Outside the courtroom, people were placing bets on the outcome. Edward was overheard telling his attorney, "I think they'll be back here in a little while and then I can go home." The jury returned a verdict of guilty of manslaughter. On October 20, 1908, Judge Cleland pronounced, "It is the sentence of this court that you serve a term of fifteen years in the state penitentiary and pay a fine of $1,000." His attorneys promised to appeal the ruling.

As Deputy Sheriff Bulger led Edward back to the jail, he told the waiting reporters:

> Even if the sentence had been only one month, I would have gone ahead with the appeal. I am not guilty of the crime and I am not willing to have the stain on my name or to serve even one month in the penitentiary. Yes, it will cost money to appeal, and my attorneys will get no more pay from the state. I will have to dig around and get some money. Since my arrest, I have never written to my father, but now I am going to write to him. I thought perhaps it would all come around right, but it has not. I do not know where my parents are, but I will communicate with my father's agent in New York, and he will send the letter to him. Yes, I think he knows of my trouble, but I have never appealed to him. I will stay right here in jail until my case is decided on appeal and will not go to Salem to begin my sentence. I believe I will get a new trial, and that in the end, it will all be right.[11]

Despite Edward's desire to stay put in the county jail, the law stated otherwise, and he found himself on the way to the Oregon State Penitentiary. Eight months into his prison term. Edward told the media that his attorneys were trying to secure a pardon from the Governor because he was a changed man. Edward wrote the following statement:

> Drug addiction! God, What horror! No word of mouth nor scratch of pen can adequately describe that cruel, merciless monster, whose almost relentless grasp holds in a thralldom infinitely worse than slavery, its millions of victims throughout the world. The far reaching effect of drug addiction can not be imagined, much less accurately determined, and only such as have had the opportunity of observing a bright intellectual and promising young man gradually lose his ambition, his character, his manhood, his all, and sink into an oblivion worse than death can understand the full import of the assertion that drug addiction constitutes a most effective barrier to the elevation of some of our brightest minds, and too frequently clouds the most brilliant intellects.[12]

Mrs. Martin visited Edward in prison on a regular basis. Edward kept busy assisting the prison officials in surveying the prison grounds using his civil engineering skills.

The one thing that always bothered the investigators was that they could never locate the murder weapon. Three years after the murder, the house Edward had lived in at the time of the murder needed to be moved to a new location to make room for a playground. As the house was lifted up, the house movers found a gun, some display rings, and envelopes with the name "Nathan Wolff." Detectives were called to the scene, and they did a thorough search once the house had been moved. They located a jeweler's polishing cloth and additional envelopes. When a reporter went to the prison to ask Edward about the items, he said, "I maintain now, as I have always maintained, that I am innocent of the crime. I am a good man now. If I am pardoned or paroled, I will be the greatest monument that could be erected to the Governor."

Six years into his fifteen-year sentence, Edward walked out of prison a free man. Governor Withycombe paroled him and released him to his father in New York.

13

Machine Gun Kelly's Ties to Medford

The day began like any other Saturday for Charles Urschel, but by the end of the day, his name would make headlines across the country. Charles was an oil tycoon who made a fortune in the oil business. He lived in Oklahoma City with his second wife, Berenice, his son, Charles, Jr., and Berenice's three children from a previous marriage—Tom, Jr., Betty, and Earl. The Urschels had married just two years before. Berenice's first husband was Tom Slick, who made a fortune as the "King of the Wildcatters." Charles was the trustee for the Slick Oil estate, valued at $23,000,000.

The Urschels invited Mr. and Mrs. Walter Jarrett to their home to play bridge the evening of Saturday, July 23, 1933. The two couples were sitting at a table on the sunporch playing bridge when suddenly two men carrying machine guns stormed the room. One of the men yelled, "Which one's Urschel?" When no answer was forthcoming, he said, "Well then come along, both of you." They were led to a large black sedan. Once inside the car, the men were forced to hand over their wallets. When one of the kidnappers looked at Walter's identification and realized he was not Charles, he was let out of the car about 10 miles outside of the city, but not before they stole $60 from his wallet.

Berenice immediately contacted the authorities when the kidnappers left with her husband. She then contacted their personal friend, E. E. Kirkpatrick. He lived in Tulsa and left immediately for the Urschel's home. Once he arrived and was apprised of the situation, he agreed to be the spokesperson for the family until Arthur Seeligson could travel from North Carolina to the Urschel's home. His first order of business was to make a public announcement asking that the kidnappers get in touch with him. He emphasized, "Our first concern is for the safe return of Mr. Urschel." He stressed that "Any sensible means of completing the transaction will be acceptable." He warned that the family would put in place measures to be positive that anyone seeking a ransom did in fact have Charles.

Once Walter was able to get to a telephone, he contacted the local law enforcement. He told them once they were in the car, the kidnappers never glanced at them or spoke to them. He told the police, "But one of those fellows surely must have spent some time getting acquainted with the streets, for he drove pretty fast." Walter mentioned that one of the men referred to his partner as Floyd, but Walter thought that was just an attempt to pin the crime on Charles "Pretty Boy" Floyd. He told the police, "When I got out of the car, I said, Urschel, I know you're hard up but try to deal with them so you won't get hurt."

Walter told the media, "If we had small pistols in our pockets, we could have plugged them both, for they didn't keep much of an eye on us. But they saw we apparently were unarmed when we were in the house." He told the reporters, the suspects treated them "like gentlemen."

Word of the kidnapping reached Washington, D.C., J. Edgar Hoover, chief of the intelligence bureau of the Department of Justice, authorized additional federal agents to go to Oklahoma and assist with the case. The secret service chief at Washington ordered the United States Department of Justice to operate the case with the highest level of censorship and the greatest degree of secrecy.

Hoover spoke to special writer for *The Oklahoma News* George Sanford Holmes:

> At least we have a very good idea as to who committed the crime. The federal government is cooperating one hundred percent with the family and state authorities and no effort will be left undone to assist in apprehending the offenders and releasing their victim.[1]

Hoover said he had been called personally by a member of the family, who requested the federal government's assistance. Hoover did not disclose the name of their suspect, but he did say it was not Charles "Pretty Boy" Floyd.

At the state level, R. H. Colvin, head of the Oklahoma State Department of Justice, was working in cooperation with federal agent Frank Smith.

They were assisted by Deputy Sheriff W. I. Eads and Clarence Hurt, a detective with the city police department. United States District Attorney Herbert Hyde was brought in as well.

The morning after the kidnapping, Berenice gave the following message to *The Oklahoma News* reporter Noel Houston:

> I am in no way interested in your capture or prosecution. I care only for the safe return of my husband. To facilitate this, I have had police withdrawn from my house and there is no one here now except our family. We are sitting beside the telephone waiting for you to call. We, just our family, have made preliminary arrangements to negotiate with you speedily and confidentially. Arthur Seeligson, my husband's closest friend, will be in charge. You can trust him. We want you to get in touch with us as soon as possible. The welfare of my husband, and his immediate return, is my only concern.[2]

As Berenice sat at the breakfast table, nervously twisting a cloth napkin, she asked Noel to relay a message to her husband, letting him know that Arthur would take care of everything.

Arthur Seeligson took the first train from Henderson, North Carolina, and arrived at the Urschel home. By the time he arrived, crowds had gathered outside the house hoping to catch a glimpse of what was happening inside. The streets surrounding the house were jammed with cars waiting their turn to drive past the house.

The family expected the suspects to contact them and make their demands known. When there was no word from the suspects on Sunday, they assumed the kidnappers were waiting for the banks to open on Monday. When there was still no word on Monday, the family became increasingly worried that Charles had been murdered.

Charles was born in Ohio and was one of four children. He worked on the family farm until he was nineteen when he moved to the city and enrolled in Oberlin Business College. He taught at a school for several years then worked as an accountant. He worked in Oklahoma and Illinois, but was interested in oil, so he moved to Oklahoma. Soon after arriving, he met Tom Slick and his sister, Flo. Charles and Flo soon married and had one son—Charles, Jr.

Tom later married a woman by the name of Berenice. They had three children, Tom Jr., Betty, and Earl. In 1930, Tom died, leaving a huge fortune. In 1931, Flo died from heart failure. As part of the Slick Oil Company, she was very wealthy when she died. A year later, Charles and Berenice married and combined their fortunes. At the time of the kidnapping, Charles was forty years old.

Finally, the kidnappers made contact with the family. They sent a letter, written by Charles, to a family friend. The letter warned Charles would be killed if they did not comply. Two days later the kidnappers sent a letter demanding $200,000. The family made arrangements with the bank and the money was delivered to Kansas City by E. E. Kirkpatrick.

Charles was released along Highway 77 near Norman. He walked to a barbeque stand, telephoned for a taxicab, and asked to be driven home. It was raining when he arrived but nothing could dampen the joy the family felt.

Later, Charles later told the reporters:

The best way to describe how I felt and must have looked upon my return home today, after my kidnapping captivity, is to tell you that the federal man stationed at the door of my home this morning, didn't recognize me and refused to let me in. I don't blame him for not knowing me as I was looking pretty haggard and seedy, I guess. It was a terrible experience and one I would not want to go through again. I was held only nine days, but it seemed to me to have been a month. I completely lost track of time. It seemed to me that there was no hope of escape or release. At times I felt my captors might grow as tired as I was of waiting and do away with the evidence by killing me. I do not know whether or not I could identify them. When they first burst into my home Saturday night a week ago while my wife and I were playing bridge with Mr. and Mrs. Jarrett, they stood in the shadows. After they put Walter Jarrett, whom they had seized with me, out of the car they blindfolded and gagged me with tape. I do not know where I was taken, but we drove without stopping for fourteen hours on the way to the hideout and about twelve hours on the way back. I could tell by the motion of the car that the trip was almost entirely over dirt roads. It seemed colder where we went. Last Wednesday when I wrote a letter home at the kidnappers' order, telling my family that my life was in danger and requesting a ransom payment, I got a peep at the place where I was being held. It looked like a three-room shanty. The two men who seized me stayed with me almost constantly, but I got the impression there were other guards and that the men holding me were working for parties higher up. My guards seldom talked, if to prevent me from recognizing their voices later, I don't know. They treated me nice enough but made it quite clear that they would not hesitate to kill me if any double-crossing put them in danger.[3]

Although the kidnappers kept Charles blindfolded, he was able to hear what was going on around him. He told the federal agents that every morning at 9:15 and every evening at 5:45, he heard an airplane fly over the house he was held captive in, with the exception of one day. The federal agents checked all airlines schedules and determined that American Airlines would have flown over Paradise, Texas, during that time.

In talking with the airline, they learned the one day that Charles did not hear the airplane was because the pilot had to change course due to bad weather. Federal agents, state agents, and city detectives from Dallas and Fort Worth combed the area and found the house where the kidnappers held Charles. They discovered Harvey Bailey, a fugitive from Kansas, asleep on a cot outside. On the cot next to him was a machine gun, an automatic rifle, and an automatic pistol. He was wanted for his role in the Kansas City Union Station Massacre wherein five men had been killed, four of whom were law enforcement officers. He had broken out of a prison in Kansas weeks earlier. He had part of the ransom money in his possession. Four other individuals at the house were arrested. Charles' fingerprints were found in the house, confirming that this had been the hideaway.

The federal agents were searching for Albert Bates for his role in the Charles' kidnapping. He was picked up in Colorado for passing bad checks. Five federal agents escorted him by plane back to Oklahoma. They were met at the airport by Sheriff Rogers, Federal Agent Colvin, six deputies armed with machine guns, and Charles Urschel. He positively identified Albert as one of his kidnappers by telling U.S. Marshall Charles Patton, "Yes, that's him, all right. He didn't have on those gold-rimmed spectacles that night, but he is the one."

Berenice added, "Oh, I'm so glad to see him like that," referring to the heavy chains and being manacled to federal agents. As the agents were getting Albert into the car, Charles walked up to him and said, "Hello, Albert." To which Albert replied, "I don't think I know you."

The serial number for each bill in the ransom money had been recorded. That information had been sent out to banks across the country. Three men were arrested in Minneapolis for trying to pass some of the ransom money.

By this time, the federal agents knew that George "Machine Gun" Kelly was the other person with Albert the night they stormed the Urschel's house. However, finding him was not easy. An intensive manhunt began covering multiple states. Federal Agent William Rorer was asleep when he received a phone call from J. Edgar Hoover informing him that Machine Gun Kelly was in Memphis, Tennessee. William was at his home in Birmingham, Alabama, but he immediately began mobilizing city, county, state, and federal officers. He arranged for two United States Army airplanes.

Machine Gun Kelly had eluded law enforcement a few weeks prior when he was spotted in San Antonio. He led agents on a chase stretching from Texas to Oklahoma, then to Arkansas, and finally to Chicago but was never captured. Machine Gun Kelly's wife, Kathryn, sent a letter days before to the United States attorney general indicating she wanted, "to live a peaceable and honorable life."

Kathryn's life was anything but peaceful the morning of September 26, 1933. Dozens of law enforcement officers stormed the house where she was staying with her husband, J. R. Tichnor, and S. E. Travis in Memphis. Sergeant Raney, armed with a sawed-off shotgun, came face to face with Machine Gun Kelly who had a revolver in his hand. Sergeant Raney said, "Drop it, Kelly."

Machine Gun Kelly dropped his weapon and placed his hands in the air saying, "I have been waiting for you all night."

Sergeant Raney replied, "Well, here we are." Detective Sergeant Floyd Wiebenga, Police Officer A. O. Clark, Federal Agent Rorer, Federal Agent B. F. Fitzsimmons, and Federal Agent R. E. Peterson arrested the other three. Department of Justice agents were flown by the United States Army from Chicago and St. Louis to assist.

Charles positively identified Machine Gun Kelly as one of the two men who stormed his house and abducted him. E. E. Kirkpatrick positively identified Machine Gun Kelly as the man he gave the satchel to that contained the ransom money.

In short order, Kathryn's parents, R. G. and Ora Shannon, and Kathryn's brother, Armon, found themselves behind bars for allowing the kidnappers to use their property in Paradise as a hideout. A trial got underway and seven people were found guilty. Machine Gun Kelly, his wife, Kathryn, Albert Bates, Harvey Bailey, R. G. Shannon, and Ora Shannon all received sentences of life imprisonment. Armon Shannon received a suspended sentence. The government recovered some of the ransom money, but they were unable to locate the entire $200,000. J. Edgar Hoover announced, "This case is not closed, and will not be closed until every cent of the ransom money has been recovered."

Medford, Oregon, is almost 2,000 miles from Oklahoma City. Yet it was here that some of the Urschel ransom money turned up. Alvin Scott, age forty-six, was driving near Winchester when he lost control of his automobile and crashed. He suffered a skull fracture along with other injuries and was hospitalized at Mercy Hospital in Roseburg. Nurses attending to Alvin removed two wallets from his clothing. When they saw the amount of cash, they became concerned and notified the police, The police in turn notified federal agents with the Bureau of Investigation out of Portland. The federal agents went to the hospital and took possession of the $1,360 that Alvin had on his person. The serial numbers on each bill were traced to the ransom money. While Alvin remained unconscious in the hospital, federal agents placed him under technical arrest.

Alvin went from a hospital bed to a jail cell cot after United States Marshal Jack Summerville escorted him to a jail in Portland. He was charged with conspiracy to aid the kidnapping plot and possessing and concealing the ransom money. The next morning, he appeared before United States Commissioner Frazer who read the list of charges against him. Alvin asked, "Am I supposed to be guilty of all that? I ain't guilty of any of that. I don't know why you got me here, or even how I got here." Commissioner Frazer was not convinced and set bail at $25,000. Upon hearing this, Alvin asked, "Can't I get out of jail to take care of my kids? I want to get out and take care of my family. I don't know anything about this other stuff. I just want to get out and look after things." His request was denied and he was held over for extradition to Oklahoma.

Alvin was the brother-in-law to Clara Feldman who married Albert Bates shortly before the kidnapping. Federal agents believed Clara, her son, Edward, and Alvin had been actively laundering the ransom money. Alvin had drawn the attention of federal agents while living in Portland the year before. They believed he had laundered approximately $46,000 in Portland. They were aware he had moved to Medford and they believed he had passed some of the bills in Medford.

While Alvin was in the hospital, federal agents, state police, and sheriff deputies went to his house in Medford. Alvin shared the house with Clara's sister, Margaret Hurtienne, and Alvin's five children, who ranged in age from ten to twenty-three years of age. Margaret had been living with them in Portland and in Medford to help with the children. Alvin had previously been married to another sister of Clara and Margaret.

The agents searched the house and the land for additional evidence. They began digging up the property or "farming it" as they referred to it as, in the hopes of uncovering more of the ransom money. Members of the Evans Creek Civilian Conservation Corps were brought to the property to assist. Their efforts paid off; they uncovered nearly $7,000 buried on the property. They also uncovered bank drafts drawn on a bank in Denver that were made payable to Clara.

Law enforcement immediately noticed a new pump house on the Alvin property. Alvin's oldest daughter, Frances, told the authorities the pump house was to be used as a washroom or a milk house. Federal agents were not convinced of that because they noticed it was wired for electricity and extra insulating paper had been placed between the wall boards and the outside of the upstairs portion of the pump house. They were concerned the pump house may have been built to hold a kidnapping victim, but they could not prove it.

In short order, Clara, her son, Edward, his bride, Betty, and Margaret were arrested and transported to Multnomah County jail. Betty was released after a short time, but the others were held for a trial.

A federal grand jury got underway in Portland with Federal Judge Edgar Vaught presiding. Alvin and Margaret were represented by Roscoe Hurst and Elton Watson. Charles and E. E. Kirkpatrick took a United Airlines flight to Portland for the court session. Charles testified that he did not recognize Alvin or Margaret. E. E. Kirkpatrick, who had gone with the banker, Lyall Barnhart, to hand over the ransom money, could not identify either of them. Lyall testified that when he prepared the ransom money, he wrote down the serial numbers of each bill. In front of the jury, Lyall identified each bill that was recovered from Alvin's yard.

During the hearing, three fruit jars were introduced into evidence that had been dug up out of Alvin's yard in Medford. Federal Agent M. B. Lindquist took the stand and explained that one jar held $4,680 in $20 Federal Reserve notes. He said the other two jars combined held seventy-three $20 Federal Reserve notes. A money bag was introduced into evidence that he said held $795 in $5 and $10 bills. He went on to say that Clara and George Davis' wedding certificate was in one of the jars along with gold pieces worth $90.

Two catholic nuns who worked as nurses at Mercy Hospital in Roseburg where Alvin was hospitalized, testified to finding "about $1500" in two wallets that Alvin had in his clothing when he was brought to the hospital. Special Agent F. A. Grimsdell of the Department of Justice told the court that the bills in the wallets matched the serial numbers of the ransom money.

The court decided there was enough evidence and that a trial should be held in Oklahoma City. Up to this point, Alvin, Margaret, Clara, and Edward had fought extradition to Oklahoma but they soon found themselves on a plane to Oklahoma accompanied by U.S. marshals.

Margaret was released from custody in Oklahoma when a true bill was not returned for her involvement. She returned to the house she shared with Alvin and helped look after his children. The others were indicted in Oklahoma.

Once a trial began in Oklahoma, more details came to light. Federal Agent C. C. Spears out of Portland testified that he assisted in digging up $44,500 of the ransom money at Clara's father's ranch in Washington. He said he was also present at the property in Medford and assisted in recovering the money buried on the property. He described locating the money in tin cans, fruit jars, vacuum jars, and other types of containers. He said Clara and Edward were helpful in pointing out areas where the money was hidden in Washington. Testimony was given about recovering $70,000 in Texas and $30,000 from Washington.

Alvin testified that he had assisted in digging up some of the ransom money near Cheyenne, Wyoming. He admitted to the court that he had purchased seven automobiles in order to launder some of the ransom money.

Clara took the stand and explained to the jury that she married Albert three months prior to the kidnapping. She admitted that she knew Albert used an alias—George L. Davis. When asked how she and her son laundered the estimated $80,000 that was Albert's share of the ransom money, she stated, "We did not know where to go. We headed for Laramie, Wyoming and then cut back toward Cheyenne. We sat in the car near a canyon until almost daybreak and then we got a cabin." She went on to say she and her son, "Acting on instructions, took the money, placed it in two thermos jugs and buried it on the highway."

Clara explained to the jury that she and Edward then drove to Chicago where they lived under assumed names and played hide and seek with the federal authorities for fifteen months. She told of making a money belt out of a towel and giving it to Edward to take to attorney Ben Laska in Denver. She said Ben later contacted her and said she owed him additional money to defend her husband. He advised her to head to Philadelphia or New York and to buy a home. Once she purchased the home, Ben told her to have a plumber build a trap underneath the drain and to store the money there. Clara said that Ben told her that was where he kept his money. She said Ben advised her to not pass any of the money at small gas stations, but instead to buy small items at stores and use larger bills to get the change in legitimate money. Clara denied knowing that Albert was involved in criminal activity prior to marrying him. When Judge Vaught asked Clara, "Did you know Bates was a criminal before you married him?" Clara, in tears, answered in the negative.

Clara pled guilty, as did her son, Edward. Alvin also pled guilty telling Judge Edgar Vaught, "We know we are guilty and want to get it over with." Charles asked the court for clemency for the trio, saying their only role was to hide Albert's share of the ransom money. Clara, Edward, and Alvin were given suspended sentences, five years' parole, and five years' probation for concealment of the ransom money. The court gave them two months to take care of their business matters in Oregon and Washington. They were required to let the state police know their whereabouts in each state. After the two months were up, they were required to return to the jurisdiction of the Oklahoma Federal Court until their sentences were finished.

In another strange twist, defense attorneys Ben Laska and James Mathers found themselves on the other side of the law. They had planned to be defense attorneys for two suspects, but instead found themselves needing defense attorneys. The two attorneys were indicted on federal charges for "illegal participation in the division of the ransom money." James had represented Harvey and Ben had represented Albert. James was acquitted for his role for receiving $1,000 of the ransom money as payment for his services. Ben was sentenced to ten years in prison for accepting $10,000 of the ransom money for providing legal services. To complicate matters even more, attorney Molly Edison, who testified on behalf of Ben, was convicted of perjury.

Charles Urschel testified in all of the trials. The Urschels took a cruise around the world after their ordeal. Machine Gun Kelly began serving his sentence at Leavenworth before being transferred to Alcatraz Island. He finished his sentence at Leavenworth, where he died. Albert and Harvey both served time at Leavenworth and at Alcatraz Island. In all, twenty people were convicted in the Urschel kidnapping.

14

The DeAutremont Brothers

The Gold Special of the Southern Pacific Railroad left Portland early on the morning of October 11, 1923. The Gold Special, also known as Train 13, was carrying mail and passengers to San Francisco. Just past noon, the train stopped at the depot in Ashland, Oregon. The passengers aboard were allowed a few minutes to stretch their legs. The train crew handed the reins over to a fresh crew from the Shasta, California, division.

The train engineer, Sidney Bates was just beginning his shift. He had been with Southern Pacific Railroad for thirty years. His fireman was twenty-three-year-old Marvin Seng. Both Sidney and Marvin made their home in Dunsmuir, California, a small town halfway between Redding, California, and the Oregon border. Marvin had worked for Southern Pacific Railroad since 1918 and had a young wife and baby at home. He was filling in for his friend, James McDonald, who had another obligation.

The brakeman coming on shift that day was Charles "Coyl" Orin Johnson who was one day shy of his thirty-eighth birthday. His wife, Ruth, was planning a party for him upon his arrival home. In the mail car was Elvyn Doughtery, who was filling in for his friend John Edwards. John had an important Masonic Lodge meeting that morning in Ashland, so he asked Elvyn to cover his shift. Elvyn had a wife, Rollie, and a four-year-old son, Raymond.

Train 13 consisted of an engine, a tender, one combination mail car, four baggage express cars, and three coaches. The mail car was made of steel and separated by a steel partition, the front was used for mail, and the back was used for pouches of mail and baggage. Elvyn was in the front and Hugh Huffy was in the back. There was a steel door they could crawl through to get from one side to the other. Beyond Hugh was the iceman, whose job was to continually ice the fish that was being transported to California to be sold to restaurants and stores.

The passengers returned to the train, having no idea they were about to make railroad history. The train began to make its way towards the Oregon–California border. At approximately 12:40 p.m., the train entered Tunnel 13. The events that transpired there soon became known the world over.

All southbound trains were required to perform a brake check prior to descending the steep Siskiyou Summit. As Sidney approached Tunnel 13, he slowed to a crawl of 5–6 miles per hour. Tunnel 13 was 3,100 feet long and constructed of timber.

What no one knew was that the DeAutremont brothers—twins Ray and Roy, age twenty-three, and their brother, Hugh, age nineteen—were hiding near the tunnel. They were planning to rob the mail car by using dynamite to gain entry. They expected to be able to steal at least $40,000, which they believed would be enough money to last the rest of their lives.

As the train slowed, Roy and Hugh jumped from their hiding spot in the bushes and climbed aboard the train. Although they had done this numerous times in the past as they traveled from one place to the next, this time they almost missed. In the middle of trying to catch the train, Roy lost his .45 pistol along the tracks. This slowed him down, and he would have missed the train completely had it not been for Hugh, who saw what happened and was able to pull Roy aboard the train. Ray was up ahead in the tunnel chain-smoking in an effort to calm his nerves.

Roy and Hugh made their way from the baggage car to the tender, where they jumped down into the engineer's cab, startlingly Sidney and Marvin. Hugh pointed his loaded shotgun at Sidney and demanded that he stop the train once the engine was barely clear of the tunnel. Hugh threatened to shoot if his demands were not met. Sidney informed Hugh that he had to turn the warning bell on as he entered the tunnel because that was company policy. Hugh reluctantly agreed to the request. Sidney did as he was told and Train 13 came to a stop inside Tunnel 13 with just its nose outside of the tunnel.

Ray was in the tunnel with a detonating device and dynamite, which he placed up against the door of the mail car. He saw Elvyn stick his head out the window in an effort to determine why the train had come to a complete stop. Ray fired his shotgun at Elvyn but missed. Elvyn quickly bolted the window and locked the safe.

Hugh Huffy was also curious why the train had come to an unexpected stop, so he peered out his door in the baggage car. From his vantage point, he could see Marvin with his hands in the air and he could see that two men were holding guns on him. Hugh Huffy quietly closed his door and waited.

The warning bell continued to clang loudly and that along with the unexpected stop made the passengers and other crewmembers begin to question what had gone wrong. The conductor of the train, C. O. Merritt, and Coyl started for the front of the train when suddenly, a tremendous explosion ripped through the tunnel. Although Ray had had some experience using dynamite, it was actually Roy who plunged the detonator. The blast took out all of the train's windows and filled the entire train and tunnel with smoke. They had wanted to denote the dynamite while the mail car was inside the tunnel so that no one would be able to hear the blast. That logic proved to be an incredible mistake because the mail car was soon engulfed in flames, and thick smoke made it impossible to see anything. Hugh ordered Sidney and Marvin back into the cab and demanded they move the train forward so the mail car would no longer be inside the tunnel.

C. O. turned back when the explosion occurred, but Coyl continued to make his way towards the mail car. In his hand, he carried a red lantern. He came upon Roy, who informed him a robbery was taking place and that his life was in great danger. Roy ordered Coyl to find Sidney and tell him to move the train forward. As Coyl began to walk towards the cab, still carrying his lantern, he startled Ray and Hugh who both fired their guns. Coyl crumbled to the ground uttering his final words, "that other fellow said to pull the thing ahead." Coyl was in great distress and Hugh shot him again.

Sidney was unable to move the train forward due to the substantial damage it had suffered. By this time, the boys were in a panic, realizing that everything was going wrong. The twins made one last attempt to get inside the mail car, but it was essentially an inferno. Elvyn died in the fire.

The brothers realized the situation was helpless and they prepared to leave this debacle of a crime scene empty handed. In a panic and not knowing what to do, Roy suddenly opened fire on Marvin, killing him instantly. Before leaving the crime scene, Ray realized that Sidney was a witness. He ordered Hugh to "bump him off and let's get out of here."

The brothers ran from the crime scene in a panic, leaving behind three knapsacks they had brought to use to haul away the money. They became disoriented and began arguing about which direction their hideout was. As they ran, they could hear the warning bell echoing throughout the countryside. The brothers finally found their shack after going in the wrong direction for a couple of miles.

Leonard and Chester Smith were on their lunch break at the Southern Pacific maintenance camp when they heard a terrific explosion. Fearing the boiler had blown on Train 13, they grabbed their fire extinguishers and headed over the summit to Tunnel 13. They were the first on the scene and they soon found a disoriented Merritt who whispered, "They all died." Realizing this was a murder scene and not a malfunction of the train, they sent one of the passengers, M. C. Micander, to run for help. He ran to the nearest operator station and asked that they send a telegraph out. The first telegraph stated "Explosion Tunnel/Train thirteen/killed several, injured many, believed to be hold-up. Please notify Associated Press."

Shortly thereafter, Jackson County Sheriff Charles Terrill received vague details of a hold up of Train 13 wherein crewmembers had been killed. He quickly formed a posse and set out for Tunnel 13. Across the California border, Sheriff Caulkins did the same thing in Siskiyou County. When the sheriffs arrived on scene, they were met by train passengers who had been trampling on the evidence. Despite this setback, Sheriff Terrill did find some evidence including a detonator machine, a .45 Colt pistol, a pair of overalls, three knapsacks, a can of black pepper, and some footpads that had been soaked in creosote. Sheriff Terrill interviewed a couple of witnesses who provided just enough information for him to be able to issue an all-points-bulletin for two men aged twenty-five to thirty, slight build, 5 feet 7 inches to 5 feet 8 inches, and 160 pounds.

Soon the Siskiyou Mountains were teaming with posses from sheriff offices from Josephine County, Coos County, Curry County, Siskiyou County, as well as Department of Justice agents, the National Guard from both Medford and Ashland, Southern Pacific Railroad special agents, prohibition officers, local game wardens, and city police. Sheriff Terrill sent for a team of Redbone hounds from Seattle to search the area for the killers.

Southern Pacific Railroad reported that "the bandits secured no loot" and all registered mail had been accounted for. They further stated that all registered mail had been in a safe that Doughtery had locked at the first sign of trouble. Later, it was reported that most letters in the mail car were wholly destroyed, but in a few cases, only the edges of the envelopes and letters had been burned. The letters that could be salvaged were sent on to the intended recipient with a note explaining what had happened.

Based on the evidence left behind, the authorities soon learned who the killers were. The grand jury of Jackson County indicted all three boys on six counts. They were charged with murder in the first degree, train robbery, robbing of the United States mail, attempted hold-up of Southern Pacific passenger train no. 13, stopping a railroad train for the purpose of committing robbery, and attempting to commit burglary in a railroad coach containing United States mail. *The Medford Mail Tribune* stated, "The murders and ruthless brutality are unparalleled in the crime history of the Northwest and the hold-up was the most sensational criminal adventure in the records of Oregon." Bench warrants were issued for Roy, Ray, and Hugh. It was ordered that they be held without bail as provided by the Oregon statutes for murder in the first degree.

Sheriff Terrill turned the investigation over to Southern Pacific Railroad Chief Special Agent Dan O'Connell, who was well known for capturing train robber Roy Gardner the year before. Within twenty-four hours, Southern Pacific Railroad posted a $2,500 reward and the United States Post Office Department (known today as the United States Post Office) posted a $5,000 reward. Wanted posters were sent all across the country. The posses continued to comb the hills without any luck. Tips poured in from neighboring communities, and as word got out, the tips began coming in from nearby states from people who were sure they had seen the train robbers.

After remaining in their hideout for ten days, the brothers decided to begin walking to the coast. The trio saw tracks from the posse and could hear airplanes overhead and knew the planes were searching for them. At night, they could see campfires in the distance and knew the men who were sitting around the fires were determined to find them. They were not dressed for the cold weather and had no provisions for it. The boys gave up their quest to reach the coast and instead headed towards California.

Once in California, the trio decided it would be better if they split up as they feared being spotted if they remained together. They chose aliases so they could write to one another care of general delivery in the towns they hoped to live in. Hugh chose the name James C. Price and headed to Santa Ana, California. Roy chose the name Johnny Johnson and told his brothers he was heading to the Sacramento area. Ray took on the alias of William B. Elliott and said he would find work on farms in Northern California. In a tearful goodbye, the brothers made plans to meet in five years on New Year's Day at the largest YMCA in New York.

Hugh did make it to Santa Ana but was disappointed there were no letters from his brothers. He stole rides on trains and made his way to Arizona, Texas, Alabama, Louisiana, and Missouri before ending up in Chicago. It was there that he saw an advertisement for the United States Army. He immediately joined up and was soon on his way to the Philippines.

After more than a year apart, the twins met up near Vacaville, California. They decided it would be best to leave the west coast and began making plans to leave California. They bounced around for a while before ending up in Ohio. In Ohio, they took on the aliases Elmer and Clarence Goodwin. They lived together and found jobs at the Wheeling Steel Company.

Ray had not been in Ohio long before he met his future wife, Hazel Sprouse. The following year, she gave birth to their son, Jackie Hugh Goodwin.

Time marched on, and despite the wanted posters that were plastered all around the world, the authorities were not able to locate the DeAutremont brothers. Yet it was now 1927 and things were about to change.

Before the infamous Alcatraz Island became a federal prison and home to some of the country's most notorious criminals such as Al Capone, Machine Gun Kelly, and Robert Stroud, it was a U.S. Army prison. It was there that Corporal Thomas Reynolds of the United States Army, Company B, 31st Infantry was stationed for a short time. One day in June 1926, he found himself with some time on his hands and he began to study a wanted poster hanging on the wall. It only took a few minutes for him to realize that the face staring back at him was that of Private Price. Thomas reported his suspicions to his supervisor, who in turn contacted the U.S. Post Office Department.

The tips had never stopped pouring in from people vying for the reward money. The Post Office inspector's office sent for more information on Private Price only to learn the U.S. Army had few details. The U.S. Post Office Department had sent officials around the globe following up on leads and this was no exception. The U.S. Post Office Department asked Inspector Fred Smith to go to Manila to determine if Private Price and Hugh DeAutremont were the same person.

On February 11, 1927, Hugh was out on the firing range when he was ordered to report to his commanding officer, Major Shearer. Hugh was introduced to Inspector Smith who began questioning Hugh as to his background and his whereabouts on October 11, 1923. Inspector Smith finally asked him point blank if he was Hugh DeAutremont. Hugh denied his true identity, forcefully stating that he was James C. Price of Pecos, Texas. Undeterred, Inspector Smith told Hugh that Corporal Reynolds was the one who had contacted the authorities. Hugh stuck by his story, claiming to be Private Price until finally the questions about his background became too much and he looked at Inspector Smith, sighed, and said, "I guess you got your man. I'm Hugh but I didn't kill anyone. Neither did my brothers."

With that, he launched into a story about being with his brothers on a hunting trip near Tunnel 13 when suddenly four men attacked them and took their clothing, their gun, and all of their money. He said they fled fearing that no one would believe them. Hugh steadfastly denied knowing the whereabouts of his brothers. In Manila, a statement was released to the media:

> On April 22, 1924 James C. Price enlisted in the United States Army in Chicago, was detailed to foreign service. He arrived in the Philippines early in 1925, being assigned to Company B, 31st Infantry. Yesterday Price was positively identified as Hugh DeAutremont at Los Banos by an Inspector of the U.S. Post Office Department aided by army authorities.[1]

The twins had not had any contact with Hugh since they parted ways in Northern California shortly after the train robbery. They had become accustomed to seeing wanted posters wherever they went and had stopped paying much attention to them. Yet one day, Ray spotted a poster that made his heart sink. The wanted poster no longer had Hugh's information on it. Ray realized that either Hugh had been captured or he was no longer alive.

About that same time, a former co-worker of the twins, Albert Collingsworth, was also studying a wanted poster. Although his eyesight was failing, he managed to do what no one else had been able to do in more than three years. He recognized the men on the poster as Elmer and Clarence Goodwin. He immediately contacted the authorities. Federal Agent Edward Pomeroy was assigned to the case.

The morning of June 8, 1927, began like any other for the twins but ended just like the nightmares that had plagued them for more than three years. Roy was at work at the Wheeling Steel Company when he was asked to report to the personnel office. As he walked in to the office, he came face-to-face with men who had spent their careers dreaming of slapping a pair of handcuffs on one of the most sought-after criminals in the world. With guns drawn, there could be no mistaking the seriousness of the situation.

Special Agent Pomeroy asked the young man seated in front of him if he was Roy DeAutremont. Roy adamantly insisted that he was Clarence Goodwin. He managed to keep this up for two hours before he broke down and admitted he was Roy DeAutremont. He sighed and simply said, "Well, it looks like some of you guys are in for a reward." He quickly stated that he had not killed anyone and that he had run because he feared no one would listen to him.

Ray was in the comfort of his home enjoying time with Hazel and Jackie Hugh, oblivious to the fact that he was in the final moments of life as a free man. He had fallen asleep in the bedroom when there was a knock at the door. Hazel opened the door to find a man who informed her Clarence had been injured at work. Ray woke from a deep slumber to hear the frightful news that Roy had been hospitalized. Ray quickly kissed Hazel goodbye and left with the stranger to go check on his brother. As Ray started to get into the waiting car, his worst nightmare came to life as he saw a car filled with men in uniforms with their guns drawn. Barely able to breathe, Ray realized that it was finally over. He had run far and long, but now it was all over. Life as a free man became a distant memory as the car sped towards the county jail.

Once at the jail, Ray tried to deny his true identity but when faced with the facts, it seemed fruitless. Finally, he uttered the words that every police officer in the nation had dreamed of hearing, "I'm Ray DeAutremont."

After a fitful night in jail, the twins were brought before Deputy U.S. Commissioner C. J. Barrow the next morning. When asked if they were Roy and Ray DeAutremont, they admitted they were. When asked if they wanted to fight extradition to Oregon, they shook their heads and quietly said no.

Many of the townsfolk in Steubenville showed up for court that morning hoping to catch a glimpse of the infamous DeAutremont brothers. Also, in court that morning was Hazel, still numb from the shock. She approached her husband as he was being led back to jail. He offered no explanation and simply said, "Goodbye Hazel." She whispered goodbye, but it was all too much for her, especially since she was pregnant with their second child.

Newspaper headlines around the world screamed that the DeAutremont brothers had been captured, thus ending a worldwide manhunt. Back in Jacksonville, Sheriff Jennings handed the newspaper to Hugh. He read the article without saying a word and then simply put the newspaper down.

By the time the handcuffs were slapped on the twins, the United States government had spent more than $500,000 in what became known as the "world's greatest manhunt" at the time. In all, more than 2,583,000 wanted posters had been printed at a cost of approximately $9,911.06.

Sheriff Jennings and his son, Chief Deputy Sheriff Louis Jennings, went by train to Ohio to collect their prisoners. As they were leaving Steubenville with the twins, they had to fight their way through a crowd estimated to be in the thousands on their way to the train depot. The twins, dressed in suits and wearing hats, played to their audience. At the depot, the crowd called out greetings and well wishes. When someone shouted, "Have a nice trip," Roy shouted back, "We wouldn't miss it for anything. Oregon's beautiful this time of year." Once on the train, they were joined by two agents from the F.B.I., two postal inspectors, and two detectives from Ohio.

As the train made its way towards Oregon, crowds of curiosity seekers gathered at every stop to catch a glimpse of the infamous twins. Once the train arrived in Oregon, reporters shouted out questions, one of which was if they had had enough to eat. Roy, enjoying the limelight, said:

Hell, if I had known the government would feed us like this, I would have given myself up long ago and no poor sap would have copped the $10,000 for squealing on us. You know Ray and I were wondering on our way out here whether or not we could have shared the reward for us if we had given ourselves up. Guess it's too late now. But I read somewhere that the government spent more than half-a-million dollars to nail us. They should have offered us a quarter-of-a-million to give up and we could have saved everyone a bundle of money.[2]

When asked about the "Siskiyou Job," it was Ray who stated:

You know we can't say anything about that. We know Hugh is going to be found innocent and we're pretty sure we can prove ourselves guiltless too, but we better wait and talk to our attorneys first. Sorry but we can't say anymore.[3]

Someone asked Ray how Hazel and the baby were. Ray said, "Well, you know I'm worried about both of them. She's only 17."

One reporter asked if what he had read in a newspaper was true; were they planning to escape to Mexico? Ray quickly stated, "No, they got it all wrong. We had just about decided to come back here, give ourselves up, and help Hughie out." One reporter asked a passenger on the train what it had been like to travel on the same train as the DeAutremonts. The passenger, W. P. Strandborg of Portland General Electric, said:

> I tell you, if I could have charged spectators 50¢ apiece each time they took my seat, I could have made enough money to pay for my ticket and got myself a Pullman. Every time I got up to go to the lavatory or dinner, ten people tried to take my place. They wanted to get a look at those guys over there. I'll bet the guards had to come out ten times a day and clear the corridor.[4]

When Sheriff Jennings was asked about the trip, he replied:

> The boys never gave us any trouble. Absolutely none. Course we had some heated discussions about various topics, but it was all in good fun. They never tried anything, but then, we didn't give them any chance either.[5]

By the time the twins arrived in Oregon, the legal process had begun for Hugh. His first trial had ended as a mistrial when a juror died unexpectedly. Hugh's second trial had wrapped up hours before the twins arrived. Hugh had been found guilty of murder in the first degree with a sentence of life imprisonment.

The three brothers reunited for the first time since they parted company in Northern California almost four years before. The joy of seeing one another soon gave way to the reason for their reunion. As the three boys discussed their future, the twins voiced their fear that the result of their trial could be death by hanging. The twins decided to confess to the murder of Marvin Seng, Coyl Johnson, Sidney Bates, and Evlyn Doughtery in exchange for a life sentence, thereby not risking the chance they could be sentenced to hang.

Judge Thomas sentenced the twins to life imprisonment and the DeAutremont brothers were taken to the Oregon State Penitentiary. Hazel and Jackie Hugh moved to Oregon briefly but then returned to Ohio where she gave birth to a son that she named Ray. Jackie Hugh grew up and worked at a manufacturing plant. Ray, Jr., served in the Korean War but took his own life after the war ended. Hazel divorced

Ray after waiting twenty-five years for him to be released. Hugh was paroled in 1958. He died of stomach cancer the following year. Roy did not do well in prison and ended up at the Oregon State Asylum where doctors performed a prefrontal lobotomy. He spent the final four years of his life in a nursing home and died in 1983. Ray was paroled after serving thirty-four years in prison. He died in 1984.

15

Constable Prescott

Llewellyn A. Banks arrived in Medford in the late 1920s with his wife, Edith, and their daughter Ruth Mae. Banks immediately began buying up orchards and investing in mining interests. It was not long before he purchased a local newspaper, *The Medford Daily News.*

In the early 1930s, the town of Medford was no different than other small towns across the country that were suffering through the Great Depression. Jobs were scarce and times were uncertain. Locally, the fruit industry was no longer able to bring in top dollar, and there was not much demand for their products. Many of the packing houses closed or cut back on the number of employees. The lumber mills were not faring any better, and they could no longer employ as many workers. Farmers in Medford and across the country were suffering from low prices, a decrease in the demand for their products, and higher transportation costs.

Perhaps it was a sign of the times that in Medford where unemployment soared and people were desperate, many were willing to listen to Llewellyn and his ideas. He used his newspaper to refer to the local politicians as "The Gang," and filled pages of his newspaper with scathing articles about the injustice suffered by the local people at the hands of the local politicians.

Llewellyn announced he would be willing to help people if they would join his newly created organization—The Good Government Congress. He touted the organization as the answer to their problems. He told the people that the purpose of the Good Government Congress was to establish justice in Jackson County. A buzz began and people joined the organization, paying dues of fifty cents per month. Llewellyn held membership meetings on the steps of the Jackson County courthouse.

Once he had his followers, Llewellyn set a plan in motion to place his own people into office during the upcoming election. He chose Gordon L. Schermerhorn as Jackson County Sheriff and M.O. Wilkins as Jackson County District Attorney. For Jackson County judge, he selected his friend Earl Fehl. Earl was the publisher of the *Pacific Record Herald* based in Medford. Earl used his newspaper to decry the local government and politicians. After the November election was held, Llewellyn was devastated to learn George A. Codding, the incumbent, had been reelected district attorney.

Soon after the election, Ralph Jennings, who had lost his bid for reelection as sheriff, filed a lawsuit asking for a recount of the ballots. He had lost by 123 votes, and both he and George began hearing rumors that something was wrong with the election.

In order for a recount to take place, the legal papers had to be served on the party who had won the election. Llewellyn ordered Sheriff-elect Gordon Schermerhorn to hide out in Northern California until January 1, when Earl Fehl would take over as county judge. As the clock struck midnight ushering in the New Year, Earl automatically became county judge. Gordon appeared at the judge's house and was sworn into office. He brought several friends with him who he swore in as deputy sheriffs. Gordon wanted his deputy sheriffs with him when he arrived at the courthouse that morning to take over the office of the Jackson County Sheriff. Sheriff Jennings quietly handed over the duties of the office, content to let the courts decide if there would be a recount of the ballots.

Llewellyn called upon his followers to insist that George, as well as Jackson County commissioner R. E. Nealon resign from office. On a cold morning in January, a rally was held outside of the Jackson County courthouse, and those in attendance were asked to sign a petition calling for the resignation of the two elected officials. Llewellyn wrote in his paper, "Unless George Codding resigns by January 12, the News calls on the citizens and taxpayers of Jackson County to establish law and order in Jackson County." Llewellyn held another rally, saying, "George Codding must be put out of office, and I don't care how you do it!" He went on to say:

Jackson County is on the verge of anarchy and chaos. I serve notice on the gang. I mean business. Either you are going to destroy me physically or I am going to drive you out of Jackson County. Someone is going to pay the penalty![1]

It was decided that Judge George F. Skipworth of Lane County would decide if a recount was necessary. Past Sheriff Jennings, through his attorneys, Porter J. Neff and Frank Van Dyke, claimed that many of the ballots with his name were cast aside for technical errors by the election boards. Testimony given during the hearing indicated the ballots had been placed in the vault in the Jackson County courthouse on December 31, 1932, and the combination to the lock had been changed.

About this time, Llewellyn's personal life was beginning to unravel. Llewellyn found himself the defendant in many lawsuits claiming he had failed to pay on promissory notes he had signed. Among the many people seeking funds was an ex-employee by the name of Eugene D. Wright. He had worked for the Medford Daily News as an advertising solicitor and was owed $250. He filed legal documents and a county clerk prepared a writ of garnishment against the assets of the newspaper. Llewellyn got word that the assets of the paper were in jeopardy so he frantically tried to hide rolls of unused newsprint before they could be seized and auctioned off to pay the debt owed to Eugene. Witnesses reported seeing two trucks from Suncrest Orchards taking newsprint to Earl's newspaper office. Constable George J. Prescott of the Medford Police Department was called upon to serve the warrant. He seized 1,200 pounds of newsprint at Llewellyn's and took it to a secure warehouse.

Llewellyn blasted the city police in his newspaper. He continually wrote that Constable Prescott had stolen $200,000 of property from him. Under the title "Banditry," he angrily declared:

Bandits on the public payrolls entered the Medford Daily News on Tuesday. Following the first outrage where bandits under the badge of authority of the law, entered a news plant and seized all the newsprint. Not content with sending officers of the law into privately owned institutions, the Medford Daily News, and there seizing illegally, newsprint and holding it illegally under dignity of our justice court.[2]

Another editorial written by Llewellyn stated:

We witness an officer entering private property and there laying his hands on and taking away property not represented by the legal documents which he held before him as legal grounds for seizing his property. We witness a Justice of the Peace hearing all of the evidence in this case, then permitting officers to retain the property which they had seized illegally.[3]

Judge William Coleman, who approved the writ of garnishment on behalf of Eugene for wages owed to him, assured the public that everything had been done legally. Charges of criminal syndicalism and criminal libel were filed. Llewellyn was indicted by the grand jury and entered a plea of not guilty before Judge Skipworth. Deputy District Attorney George Neilson advised the court that a request had been filed with the governor asking that a special prosecutor be appointed. The court agreed saying the special prosecutor should be, "In no way involved with your difficulty here."

On Monday afternoon, February 20, 1933, Judge Skipworth ruled that a recount of the election ballots was legal and should begin the following morning. Llewellyn was quoted as saying, "The ballots must not see the light of day, or I might as well leave Jackson County for Ralph Jennings will be the sheriff." He called upon his "inner circle." Then he called for an emergency meeting of the Good Government Congress. He requested they report to the courthouse that evening. Llewellyn roared, "There has been a breakdown in law and order and a miscarriage of truth." He declared he would kill any police officer who tried to arrest him. In an ominous tone, Llewellyn cried out that "Jackson County's troubles will never be solved peacefully." He told his audience of 1,000 members that he had written to the governor and to the Supreme Court warning them, "Unless justice is restored, I will take the field in revolution."

The weather was cold and overcast the next morning as the townsfolk headed off to work. Those tasked with the recount of the election ballots awoke knowing they had a busy day ahead of them. Attorney Elton Watkins of Portland, representing Schermerhorn, Attorney Frank Van Dyke, representing Jennings, Attorney Frank DeSousa, and locksmith Charles Fischer met at the courthouse to begin the arduous task of recounting the ballots. Charles was there to unlock each ballot pouch. The men were walking behind the courthouse when one of them noticed a broken window. Upon investigation, they noticed it went to the basement. They immediately went inside the courthouse and down to the basement where the vault was kept. County Clerk George R. Carter opened the door to the vault. As the men peered into the vault, it was obvious that someone had stolen thousands of election ballots. The police descended on the courthouse and secured fingerprints from the crime scene. They began interviewing those who had been at the courthouse the prior evening. Some recalled sensing they were being watched, others spoke of having a feeling of uneasiness sweep over them, but no one could pinpoint the reason. Some witnesses remembered men just sulking about in the shadows, but no one had any real answers.

Upon learning of the theft of the ballots, Judge Skipworth, who was to oversee the recount, ordered a dismissal of the action of a recount on the grounds that the vital evidence was missing, and even if found, would be useless.

The authorities estimated more than 10,000 election ballots had been stolen, representing districts from all of Jackson County. Knowing how heavy and cumbersome each pouch was, it was quickly decided this was the work of more than one person. Upon further investigation, they just as quickly concluded this had to have been an inside job. Detective Sergeant James R. O'Brien, with the Oregon State Police, was assigned to the case. With a keen eye, he observed a tiny shred of fabric still clinging to the broken window. Detective Sergeant O'Brien spoke to County Clerk George Carter, who was in charge of the vault. County Clerk Carter informed him that two brothers, Mason Sexton, age twenty, and Wilbur Sexton, age seventeen, had assisted him with the vault the day of the theft. He explained that the brothers had been arrested on New Year's Eve during a brawl and were lodged in the county jail on the top floor of the courthouse. When it came time for their court trial, the grand jury returned "Not a True Bill" and they were free to go. Yet, they did not leave the courthouse. Some of the county workers wondered why the boys were now living at the jail and receiving "room and board." Others noticed the boys circulating literature and soliciting new members for the Good Government Congress. The grand jury decided to investigate, but nothing came of the investigation prior to this nocturnal theft.

Upon learning of this information, Detective Sergeant O'Brien asked Chief of the Medford Police Department Clatous McCredie to walk among the crowds who had gathered at the courthouse to see if he could spot the Sexton brothers. Sure enough, there was a shabbily dressed man whose pants were not only torn but the material matched the evidence left behind. When questioned, neither brother was willing to talk. They were shown the fragment of cloth found at the crime scene that matched Mason's pants, but still they remained silent. Finally, after four days of being questioned, Mason proclaimed, "I'll talk and talk plenty." Mason and Wilbur's confessions filled fourteen pages.

The Sexton brothers explained that Sheriff Schermerhorn and Judge Fehl gave the boys permission to live at the courthouse in exchange for securing additional members for the Good Government Congress. They recalled on the night in question, they were wandering the halls when they came upon their father talking to Judge Fehl, Chief County Jailer John Glenn, Deputy Sheriff Charles Davis, county road supervisor and mayor of the town of Rogue River Walter Jones, vice-president of the Good Government Congress C. J. Connors, and Ashland ward leader of the Good Government Congress Thomas Brecheen.

They were asked if they knew the combination to the vault. When they replied they did not, the men questioned them about how they could gain access through the rear window. They explained that there was a collapsible steel shutter inside the window but it was not in use at the time. Judge Fehl asked if they were positive and when they replied in the affirmative, he left the group and went to the meeting of the Good Government Congress. The other men went to the boiler room and grabbed a crowbar. Then they went outside and attempted to pry the window open. When that failed to work, they returned to the boiler room, selected a monkey wrench, went back outside, and Mason proceeded to smash the window. In order to drown out the noise of the breaking glass, Mayor Jones asked R. C. Cummings to start his Ford automobile, which he did. The boys estimated there were twelve to fourteen men hauling the ballot pouches to vehicles that were waiting in the darkness. The boys recalled seeing Sheriff Schermerhorn standing in the shadows of the courthouse, observing the theft of the ballots. Once the ballots were loaded into the cars, they sped off towards the Rogue River. Each pouch was then stuffed with rocks and thrown into the river.

The Sexton brothers returned "home" to the courthouse and were surprised to find Thomas still there. Thomas told them they would need to steal more pouches and while they were doing that, he would go down to the Medford Daily News and borrow a car. When Thomas failed to return, the boys got nervous and decided to toss the pouches into a furnace at the courthouse.

The next day, they saw Sheriff Schermerhorn in the hallway of the courthouse. He admonished them to not say a word to anyone, not even to their mother, or they would be in a lot of trouble. The boys said Glenn had promised them $10 each and a job at the courthouse for their part in the crime. The boys later learned that some of the other participants had burned their ballots in their own stoves at home.

O'Brien recovered the tools used in the break-in. Under a microscope, he found evidence they had been used in the crime. Sergeant E. E. Walker of the Game Division of the Oregon State Police along with Officers Roach, Malcolm, and Levya retrieved four pouches of election ballots from the Rogue River. The authorities also found evidence of burned ballots in the furnace of the courthouse.

District Attorney Codding quickly prepared arrest warrants for those known to have been involved with this outrageous crime. For those whose names were not yet known, warrants were drawn up for "John Doe."

One of the most challenging arrests was that of the sheriff. Only the governor of Oregon or a coroner could arrest a sheriff. Sheriff Schermerhorn was lured to the offices of the Oregon State Police. Once there, he was invited into O'Brien's office. Suddenly, the coroner appeared and placed him under arrest for burglary not in a dwelling. The others were rounded up with the exception of Judge Fehl, who they believed had been tipped off and had left town.

Five days after the theft, the police received a tip that Judge Fehl was back on the bench. Constable Prescott and Detective Sergeant O'Brien loaded their pockets with tear gas bombs and headed to the courthouse. As they entered the courtroom, they were greeted with threats by members of the Good Government Congress. They read Judge Fehl the arrest warrant and took him away in handcuffs.

A top member of the Good Government Congress, Wesley McKitrick, came forward with information. He explained that Sheriff Schermerhorn planned to deputize 250 members of the Good Government Congress so that they could arrest every city police officer and transport them to an abandoned mining bunkhouse deep in the woods. They would then arrest District Attorney Codding and Judge Norton and take them up in the hills and hang them. Wesley said he had been promised a position of captain when this plan was completed. He further stated he had been busy selecting the men who would be deputized and the plan was close to fruition.

The afternoon of March 15, 1933, a grand jury handed down thirty-two indictments, including an indictment for Llewellyn A. Banks. He could now be arrested on the charge of burglary not in a dwelling and for criminal syndicalism for his mastermind plan of the theft of election ballots. The arrest of Llewellyn was possible based on the information Wesley included in his nineteen-page confession. The grand jury also indicted Judge Fehl and Sheriff Schermerhorn on additional charges relating to the theft of the election ballots.

The next morning, Constable Prescott, Detective Sergeant O'Brien, Oregon State Police Sergeants C. A. Warren, and A. K. Lumsden went to Llewellyn's house to make the arrest. Detective Sergeant O'Brien knocked on the front door. Mrs. Banks opened it a crack and while they were explaining the arrest warrant, Llewellyn opened fire, instantly killing Constable Prescott.

Llewellyn and his wife, Edith, were arrested and charged with murder in the first degree. A jury trial was held and they returned a verdict of murder in the second degree for Llewellyn. The other charges pending against Llewellyn—criminal syndicalism, criminal libel, and the theft of the ballots—were dismissed. Edith was acquitted.

Thomas Breechen, the Ashland ward leader of the Good Government Congress, pled guilty. He was sentenced to eighteen months in the Oregon State Penitentiary. Ex-Mayor Walter Jones was sentenced to four years at the Oregon State Penitentiary, as was Llewellyn's business manager, Arthur LaDieu. The Sexton brothers received probation. The vice president of the Good Government Congress, C. Jean Connors, appeared before Judge Skipworth. Despite the tears running down his face, he found out he was heading to prison. Ex-Sheriff Schermerhorn was sentenced to three years in prison. Judge Fehl received a sentence of four years in prison. R. C. Cummings, Earl Bryant, and James Gaddy, who all pled guilty, were placed on parole for two years.

Virgil Edington, a young man from the nearby town of Gold Hill, summed up his involvement in the ballot theft by saying, "We were all bamboozled by Banks and thought stealing the ballots would be a heroic stunt and in no way a crime."

All told, the cost of all trials was estimated at between $25,000 and $30,000—a hefty price for any county to bear during the Great Depression.

Edith and Ruth moved to Salem to be near Llewellyn, then later to Monrovia, California. They lived together in an apartment until Edith died in 1967. Ruth worked as a librarian during her career. On September 22, 1945, Llewellyn A. Banks died alone in his jail cell after serving twelve years. Constable Prescott's wife, Lottie, died in 1962 at the age of eighty.

Endnotes

Chapter 1

  1 *The Bend Bulletin*, April 25, 1924, p. 1.

Chapter 3

  1 Stone, S. A., *The Capital Journal*, September 19, 1952, p. 1.

Chapter 4

  1 *The Statesman Journal*, December 16, 1931, p. 10.
  2 *The Statesman Journal*, June 23, 1932, p. 3.
  3 Thomas, D., *The Capital Journal*, December 18, 1951, p. 1.

Chapter 5

  1 *The News Review*, January 18, 1923, p. 1.
  2 *Grants Pass Courier*, January 19, 1923, p. 8.
  3 *Medford Mail Tribune*, August 18, 1925, p. 1.
  4 *The Capital Journal*, August 18, 1925, p. 5.
  5 *Ibid.*, p. 8.
  6 *Albany Democrat*, August 20, 1925, p. 1.
  7 *The News Review*, August 18 1925, p. 1.
  8 *Morning Register*, August 19, 1925, p. 4.
  9 *Ibid.*
10 *Ibid.*
11 *Ibid.*
12 *Ibid.*
13 *The News Review*, August 18, 1925, p. 7.
14 *Spokane Chronicle*, August 19, 1925, p. 2.

15 *The Capitol Journal*, August 18, 1925, p. 1.
16 *The Evening Herald*, August 20, 1925, p. 1.
17 *The Capital Journal*, August 17, 1925, p. 8.
18 *The Evening Herald*, August 22, 1925, p. 5.
19 *The Statesman Journal*, August 23, 1925, p. 5.
20 *Ibid.*
21 Upjohn, D., *The Capitol Journal*, April 20, 1928, p. 6.

Chapter 8

1 *The Oregon Statesman*, November 10, 1923, p. 1.
2 *The Spokesman-Review*, October 23, 1923, p. 4.
3 *Albany Evening Herald*, December 15, 1923, p. 1.
4 *Ibid.*
5 *Ibid.*

Chapter 9

1 *The Statesman Journal*, June 10, 1902, p. 4.
2 *Ibid.*, p. 3.
3 *The Wichita Beacon*, July 12, 1902, p. 9.
4 *Ibid.*
5 *The Statesman Journal*, June 11, 1902, p. 1.
6 *The Statesman Journal*, June 10, 1902, p. 1.
7 *The Weekly Gazette*, June 25, 1902, p. 1.
8 *The Tacoma Daily Ledger*, July 7, 1902, p. 4.
9 *The Statesman Journal*, July 3, 1902, p. 1.
10 *Ibid.*
11 *The Spokesman-Review*, August 11, 1902, p. 10.

Chapter 10

1 *The News-Review*, July 15, 1921, p. 3.
2 *The Tacoma Daily Ledger*, July 20, 1921, p. 3.
3 *Ibid.*
4 *Ibid.*
5 , August 13, 1921, p. 1.
6 *Portland Telegram*, August 13, 1921, p. 1.
7 *The News Review*, October 4, 1921, p. 6.
8 *The News-Review*, October 20, 1921, p. 1.
9 *Ibid.*

Chapter 12

1 *The Statesman Journal*, May 2, 1908, p. 1.
2 *The Idaho Statesman*, September 1, 1905, p. 8.
3 *The Oregon Daily Journal*, May 6, 1908, p. 1.
4 *The Statesman Journal*, May 6, 1908, p. 1.
5 *Ibid.*
6 *The Capitol Journal*, May 5, 1908, p. 10.

7   *The Oregon Daily Journal*, May 6, 1908, p. 3.
8   *Ibid.*
9   *Ibid.*
10   *Ibid.*
11   *The Oregon Daily Journal*, October 20, 1908, p. 1.
12   *The Oregon Daily Journal*, June 6, 1909, p. 55.

Chapter 13

1   Holmes, G. S., *The Oklahoma News,* July 24, 1933, p. 1.
2   *The Oklahoma News,* July 24, 1933, p. 1.
3   *Pittsburg Sun-Telegraph*, August 1, 1933, p. 11.

Chapter 14

1   *Evening Star*, February 12, 1927, p. 1.
2   *Morning Register*, June 21, 1927, p. 1.
3   *Ibid.*
4   *Medford Mail Tribune*, June 21, 1927, p. 11.
5   *Medford Mail Tribune*, June 21, 1927, p. 1.

Chapter 15

1   *Medford Mail Tribune*, January 12, 1933, p. 1.
2   *The Medford Daily News* February 9, 1933, p. 1.
3   *Ibid.*

Bibliography

Albany Democrat, August 20, 1925.

Albany Evening Herald, December 15, 1923.

Evening Star, February 12, 1927.

Grants Pass Courier, January 19, 1923.

Holmes, G. S., *The Oklahoma News*, July 24, 1933.

Medford Mail Tribune, August 18, 1925; June 21, 1927; and January 12, 1933.

Morning Register, August 19, 1925 and June 21, 1927.

Pittsburg Sun-Telegraph, August 1, 1933.

Portland Telegram, August 13, 1921.

Spokane Chronicle, August 19, 1925.

Stone, S. A., *The Capital Journal*, September 19, 1952.

The Bend Bulletin, April 25, 1924.

The Capital Journal, May 5, 1908; August 17, 1925; and August 18, 1925.

The Evening Herald, August 20, 1925 and August 22, 1925.

The Idaho Statesman, September 1, 1905.

The Medford Daily News February 9, 1933.

The News Review, July 15, 1921; August 13, 1921; October 4, 1921; October 20, 1921; January 18, 1923; and August 18 1925.

The Oklahoma News, July 24, 1933.

The Oregon Daily Journal, May 6, 1908; October 20, 1908; and June 6, 1909.

The Oregon Statesman, November 10, 1923.

The Spokesman-Review, August 11, 1902 and October 23, 1923.

The Statesman Journal, June 10, 1902; June 11, 1902; July 3, 1902; May 2, 1908; May 6, 1908; August 23, 1925; December 16, 1931; and June 23, 1932.

The Tacoma Daily Ledger, July 7, 1902 and July 20, 1921.

The Weekly Gazette, June 25, 1902.

The Wichita Beacon, July 12, 1902.

Thomas, D., *The Capital Journal*, December 18, 1951.

Upjohn, D., *The Capitol Journal*, April 20, 1928.